George Robert Parkin

Round the empire for the use of schools

The Earl of Rosebery

George Robert Parkin

Round the empire for the use of schools
The Earl of Rosebery

ISBN/EAN: 9783337173739

Printed in Europe, USA, Canada, Australia, Japan

Cover: Foto ©Andreas Hilbeck / pixelio.de

More available books at **www.hansebooks.com**

ROUND THE EMPIRE

"Thou who of Thy free grace didst
build up this Britannick Empire to a
glorious and enviable heighth, with all
her Daughter Ilands about her, stay us
in this felicitie."

JOHN MILTON.

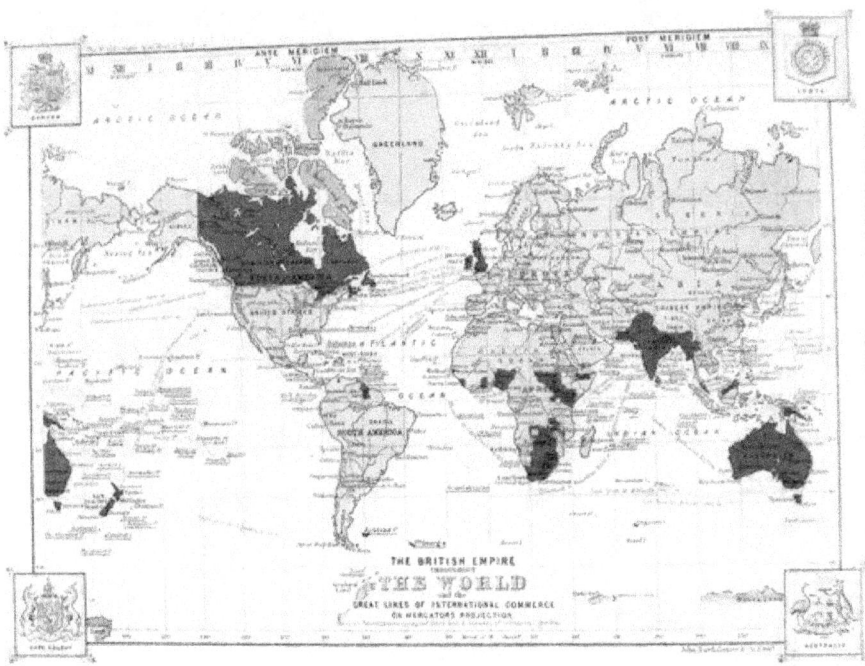

THE BRITISH EMPIRE
THROUGHOUT
THE WORLD
and the
GREAT LINES OF INTERNATIONAL COMMERCE
ON MERCATORS PROJECTION

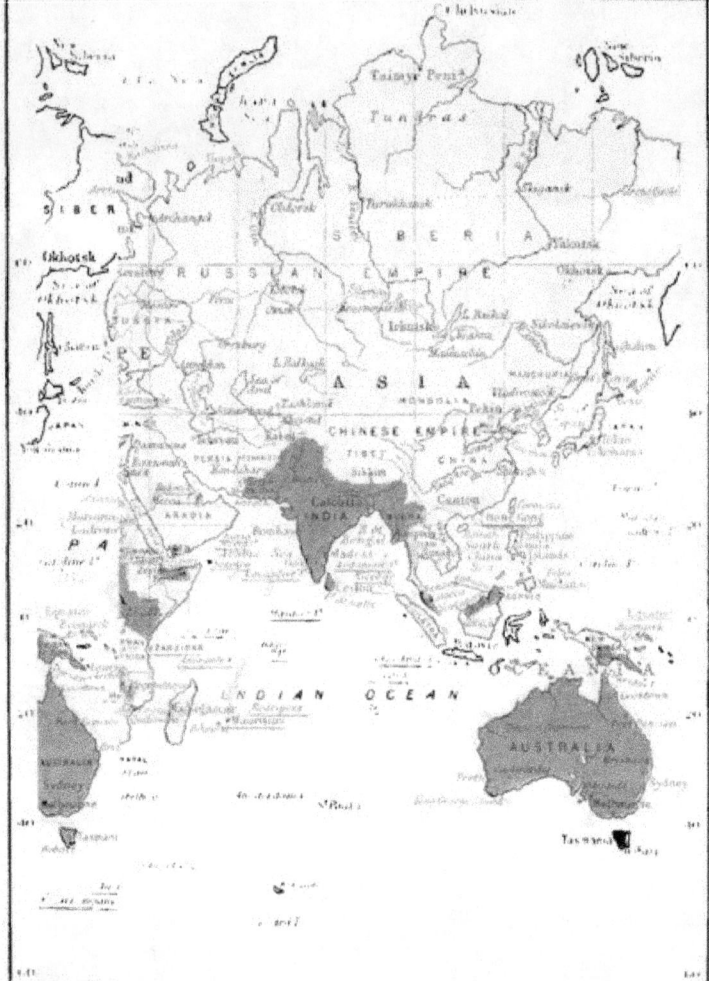

Round the Empire

FOR THE USE OF SCHOOLS

BY

GEORGE R. PARKIN, M.A.

WITH A PREFACE BY

The Right Hon. The EARL OF ROSEBERY, K.G.

133rd THOUSAND
(REVISED)

TORONTO:
THE COPP, CLARK CO., LIMITED
LONDON:
CASSELL AND COMPANY, LIMITED

PREFACE.

I HAVE been asked to write a line of introduction to this book, and gladly comply, as its primary purpose is to remind our children that they inhabit not an island but an Empire. There are few political facts, perhaps none, that should exercise so great an influence on their future lives.

For a collection of States spread over every region of the earth, but owning one head and one flag, is even more important as an influence than as an Empire. From either point of view it is a world-wide fact of supreme significance; but in the one capacity it affects only its own subjects, and in the other all mankind. With the Empire statesmen are mainly concerned; in the influence every individual can and must have a part. Influence is based on character, and it is on the character of each child that grows into manhood within British limits that the future of our Empire rests.

If we and they are narrow and selfish, averse to labour, impatient of necessary burdens, factious and self-indulgent: if we see in public affairs not our Empire but our country, not our country but our parish, and in our parish our house, the Empire is doomed. For its maintenance requires work and sacrifice and intelligence.

If, on the other hand, we aim at the diffusion of the blessings of industry undisturbed by war, if we aim at peace secured, not by humiliation but preponderance, we need to preserve our Empire not for ourselves only but for mankind. And this is said not pharisaically, not to the exclusion of other countries, but because ours is the most widely spread and the most penetrating of nationalities. The time, indeed, cannot be far remote when the British Empire must, if it remain united, by the growth of its population and its ubiquitous dominion, exercise a controlling authority in the world. To that trust our sons are born.

I hope, then, that the youth of our race will learn from this book how great is their inheritance and their responsibility. Those outside these islands may learn the splendour of their source and their " home," as well as communion with the other regions under the Crown of Great Britain ; and within, English, Scottish, and Irish children may learn not to be shut in their shires, but that they are the heirs of great responsibilities and a vast inheritance. History has marked those that made this Empire, and will mark, with equal certainty but in a different spirit, those who unmake it or allow it to dissolve.

Mr. Parkin, the author of this book, whose earnest eloquence is inspired by a single zeal, pursues the picturesque and instructive method of a tour round the British Empire. He himself is best known as the untiring advocate of a cause which represents the high resolve to maintain Imperial unity. But in this book there is put forward no theory, no constitution, and no plan. He probably believes, as most of us do, that the security for national union lies not so much in Parliamentary projects as in the just appreciation of Imperial responsibility. Such a cause can only be furthered and fostered by this little book.

ROSEBERY.

London, Feb., 1892.

CONTENTS.

CHAPTER I.

LEAVING THE OLD COUNTRY.

PAGE

The British Empire—The Ocean Empire—Oceans do not Divide—Shortening Time is equal to Shortening Distance—British Citizenship—The Variety of the Empire—Round the Empire—Crossing the Ocean. Good-bye—The Mouth of the Mersey—The Flags of the Nations—Outward Bound—The Mails—Fellow Passengers—Emigration—Why People Emigrate—Land Ahead! Newfoundland—The Short Cut across the Atlantic—The St. Lawrence—The Southern Route—New Friends under Old Names—From Ocean to Ocean by Rail ...   1

CHAPTER II.

THE GREAT DOMINION.

The Size of Canada—How Canada became a Part of the Empire—How Canada has been kept for the Empire—The "Loyalists"—Self-Government for the Colonies—Canadian Confederation...   28

CHAPTER III.

THE PHYSICAL FEATURES OF CANADA.

The Waterways of the Dominion—A Wonderful Picture—Natural Divisions—The Climate of Canada—The Canadian Winter ...   36

CHAPTER IV.

THE PROVINCES OF CANADA AND THEIR PRODUCTS.

Political Divisions—The Maritime Provinces—Nova Scotia—New Brunswick—The Bay of Fundy—A Ship Railway—Prince Edward Island—The Acadians—Quebec and the French Canadians—Ontario—"Lumbering"—Cutting up the Timber—Maple Sugar—Manitoba—The North-West Territories—Free Lands—British Columbia—A Picture of the Pacific Coast—The Products of British Columbia—The Great Fur Land   45

CHAPTER V.
THE ATLANTIC COAST.

PAGE

Newfoundland and Labrador—The "French Shore"—The Newfoundland Fisheries—Labrador—Bermuda—The West Indies—Climate of the West Indies—Slavery—Coolie Labour—"Black and White" in the West Indies—The Groups of Islands—What we get from the West Indies—The Bahamas—Jamaica—The Leeward Islands—The Windward Islands—Trinidad—Confederation of the West India Islands—British Honduras—British Guiana—El Dorado—The Falkland Islands   74

CHAPTER VI.
THE PACIFIC COAST.

Vancouver—The Canadian Pacific Railway—The Shortest Route to the Far East—Across the Pacific—A Lost Day—An Empire upon which the Sun never sets—The Pacific Cable—The Fiji Islands—The Odds and Ends of the Empire   94

CHAPTER VII.
AUSTRALASIA—NEW ZEALAND.

The South Temperate Zone—New Zealand—A Second England—The History of New Zealand—The Maories—Facts about New Zealand—New Zealand Mutton—Other New Zealand Products—Gold in New Zealand—Towns and Harbours of New Zealand   105

CHAPTER VIII.
AUSTRALASIA—TASMANIA.

Tasmania—Tasmanian Fruit in England—Other Tasmanian Products   118

CHAPTER IX.
THE AUSTRALIAN CONTINENT—NEW SOUTH WALES.

Australia—First Settlement of Australia—Canada and Australia compared—The Southern Cross—Divisions of Australia—New South Wales—Sydney—Australian Wool—Sheep Runs and Squatters—The Squatter's Enemies   ...   122

CHAPTER X.
THE AUSTRALIAN CONTINENT—VICTORIA.

Victoria—Gold—The Rush to the "Diggings"—Gold Mining at the Present Day—Australian Naval Defence   133

CHAPTER XI.

THE AUSTRALIAN CONTINENT—SOUTH AUSTRALIA.   PAGE

South Australia—Products of South Australia—"Broken Hill"—
South Australian Explorers—How Melbourne talks to London   142

CHAPTER XII.

THE AUSTRALIAN CONTINENT—WESTERN AUSTRALIA AND
QUEENSLAND.

Western Australia—Queensland—Products of Queensland—Mount
Morgan—Sugar—Cattle Runs—The Barrier Reef—Water
Supply and Irrigation in Australia—Homeward Routes from
Australia   147

CHAPTER XIII.

AFRICA.

Africa—The Race for Africa—Climate and Colonisation in Africa—
Cape Colony—Dutchmen, Englishmen, and Natives—Climate
and Products of South Africa—The Great Karroo—Ostrich
Farming   155

CHAPTER XIV.

AN AFRICAN INDUSTRY.

A Visit to an Ostrich Farm   164

CHAPTER XV.

BRITISH POSSESSIONS IN AFRICA.

Mohair—Diamonds—Natal—Protectorates and Crown Colonies—
The Transvaal and the Orange River Colony—Trading
Companies in Africa—Portuguese Territory—The Duty
of the British Government—West Africa—Sierra Leone
—St. Helena—Ascension   169

CHAPTER XVI.

BRITISH STRONGHOLDS IN THE MEDITERRANEAN.

The Mediterranean Sea—Gibraltar—Malta—Cyprus—The Suez
Canal—The Passage through the Canal—The Value of the
Canal—Aden—Perim and Socotra   186

CHAPTER XVII.

INDIA.

The Road to India—India—The English in India—The Population
of India—The History of Divided India—The East India

Company—English and French in India—India as We found PAGE
it—Sepoys—India under the Company—India under the
Crown—The Sepoy Mutiny—The Empress of India   ...   201

CHAPTER XVIII.
PHYSICAL FEATURES OF INDIA.

Geography of India—The Mountain Region—The River Plains—
The Deccan—Burmah—Ceylon...   ..   211

CHAPTER XIX.
BRITISH RULE IN INDIA.

The Defence of India—Indian Trade—India's Tribute to Britain—
What England does for India—Famine—Our Good Work in
India   219

CHAPTER XX.
THE NATIVE STATES OF INDIA.

British and Native States   228

CHAPTER XXI.
BRITISH POSSESSIONS IN EASTERN SEAS.

Asiatic Colonies — Singapore — Penang and Malacca — Borneo
Labuan, &c.—Sarawak and Raja Brooke—Hong-Kong—
New Guinea—Mauritius—The Seychelles—Rodrigues   ...   230

CHAPTER XXII.
TRADE OF THE EMPIRE.

The Great Trade Routes of the Empire—How we Defend the Trade
Routes—Coal and Coaling Stations—Coal on the Trade
Routes—Coal on the Atlantic—Coal on the North Pacific—
Coal on the South Pacific—H.M.S. *Calliope*—Coal in India
and South Africa—Telegraphic Cables—Atlantic Cables—
Eastern Cables—Cables to the Cape   241

CHAPTER XXIII.
HOW OUR COLONIES ARE GOVERNED.

Self-Governing Colonies—Crown Colonies—Colonies with Repre-
sentative Institutions—The India Office—The Colonial Office
—The Foreign Office—How the Colonies are represented in
England—The Building of the Empire—Home   ...   255

INDEX   264

INTRODUCTION.

THIS book has been written with the object of giving to boys and girls in our elementary schools a simple and connected account of those parts of our great Empire which are outside of the British Islands, and in which so many of them are likely to find homes.

Within the limits of a small volume only the broadest outlines of a subject so vast can be drawn. General statistics, and such as seem likely to leave a distinct impression on the memory, have alone been given.

Special attention has been directed to grouping facts in such a way that their bearing upon the life of the nation may be easily grasped by young minds, and the closeness of the connection which exists between the industries and interests of our people abroad and of those who remain at home has been indicated as often as possible by familiar illustrations.

For the performance of the ordinary duties of citizenship it is every day becoming more essential that all British people should understand clearly the relation to each other of the various portions of their vast national domain.

Our children cannot begin the study of the subject too soon; our statesmen and thinkers can scarcely pursue it too far.

It is hoped that this little volume may find its way into many schools, and prove helpful to teachers who are interested in building up British patriotism on that basis of wider knowledge which is necessitated by the wonderful facts of our national growth.

ROUND THE EMPIRE.

The British Empire.

THE British Islands, in which we live, cover a very small part of the surface of the earth. But the British Empire, of which these islands are the centre, covers a very large part of that surface—much larger than was ever held by any nation except our own.

The diagram on the following page shows how small in area the United Kingdom is when compared with some of the other great divisions of the Empire.

It is only about one-thirtieth of the size of Canada, one-twenty-fifth of the size of Australia, one-eleventh of the size of India. All the land in England, Wales, Scotland, and Ireland is only about an eightieth part of that which British people have occupied, or rule over, in different parts of the world.

It is difficult even to form in the mind a clear idea of the great size of the Empire of which the United Kingdom is a part. It embraces nearly one-half of North America, a small part of South America, the whole of Australia, New

B

Zealand, and Tasmania, a vast extent of territory in different parts of Africa, and in Asia—a country which supports a population of 286 millions of people.

CANADA
3,043,711 Square Miles
AUSTRALIA
(COMMONWEALTH)
2,972,573 Square Miles
INDIA
1,559,603 Square Miles
RHODESIA
264,000 Square Miles
CAPE COLONY
1?1,416 Square Miles
UNITED KINGDOM
120,979 Square Miles
TRANSVAAL
11?,139 Square Miles
NEW ZEALAND
104,471 Square Miles
ENGLAND & WALES
58,309 Square Miles
ORANGE RIVER COL.
43,326 Square Miles
IRELAND
32,583 Square Miles
BORNEO
31,106 Square Miles
SCOTLAND
3?,7?5 Square Miles
NATAL
29,200 Square Miles

FIG. 1.—DIAGRAM SHOWING COMPARATIVE AREAS OF THE UNITED KINGDOM AND PRINCIPAL COUNTRIES WITHIN THE EMPIRE.

If we add to these the islands we possess in the East and West Indies, and others scattered throughout the Atlantic, Pacific, and Indian Oceans, we find that the British Empire actually comprises only a little less than one-fifth of the land surface of the globe.

This immense area is inhabited by rather more than one-fifth of the whole estimated population of the world.

The Ocean Empire.

In addition to its remarkable size and vast population the Empire has another special characteristic which we should observe with attention.

It is sometimes called *An Oceanic Empire*, and there is, perhaps, no single phrase which expresses so well the most marked point of difference between it and other large States. All the great oceans wash its shores. Water, more than land, forms its boundaries, and the sea is the chief means of connection between its different parts. A larger proportion of its people finds employment on the sea than is the case in other countries. The ocean trade of its people is greater than that of any nation of present or past times. British ships not only carry British commerce, but also a large part of the merchandise exchanged between other countries. We are almost as much interested in keeping safe the great ocean highways over which these ships pass as in guarding the streets of our cities in which traffic is daily going on.

We see therefore that the expression "oceanic" means a great deal when applied to the British Empire. Indeed, the greatness and prosperity of the State to which we belong seem to depend as much upon our connection with the sea as upon the extensive possessions of land of which we have spoken. It is impossible to understand the British Empire and its relation to other States unless we constantly keep in mind how much of its interests are upon the ocean.

We are accustomed to speak of the ocean as separating countries or continents from each other. Before people understood the art of navigation this was quite true, and it still seems to be so. But great changes have taken place which make the separation caused by the ocean more apparent than real.

Oceans do not Divide.

It is very necessary, therefore, that people who inhabit the different parts of an Empire so widely scattered as ours should understand that, in many ways, oceans do not divide.

For **trading** purposes, particularly, the ocean is much more a uniter than a divider. Goods are carried much more cheaply by sea than by land. It costs no more to bring wheat by sea from Montreal or New York to London, a distance of 3,500 miles, than to bring the same quantity by rail from some of the English counties to London.

It costs about the same price to carry a bale of wool from London to Yorkshire, a distance of about two hundred miles, as to bring it fully 12,000 miles by water from New Zealand to London.

An ironmaster pays as much to have his heavy iron goods carried from the Midland Counties to Liverpool as from Liverpool to the farthest parts of the world. So in many ways we find, when we want to send goods abroad, or to get back the products of other countries, that the ocean, instead of dividing, really furnishes the easiest and cheapest means of intercourse. The great woollen, cotton,

iron, and other manufactures in this country, which give
work to so many millions of our people, could not be so
extensive as they are were it not for the cheapness with
which food for the workers, and the cotton, wool, and other
materials used in manufacture, can be brought by sea from
the ends of the earth, and goods sent back again. The
people of a great trading nation such as ours is should
get rid of the idea that oceans divide.

Shortening Time is Equal to Shortening Distance.

It is true that we cannot shorten space, but we can
shorten time, and in point of time oceans now separate
much less than they did fifty years ago. We cross the
Atlantic with steamships in as many days as it once took
weeks by sailing vessels. Many thousands of people cross
every year to transact business or to spend a few weeks'
holiday on either side. Britain and Australia are less than
thirty days apart, and every week great steamships laden
with goods and passengers start from one to the other.

This is not all. The telegraph wire stretches under
the sea as well as over the land, and puts remote parts of
the world into almost instant touch with each other. You
can send a message to Canada or Australia and get an
answer in a few hours, or even in a few minutes. The
morning or evening papers in Melbourne or Montreal have
in them every day a great deal of the same news from
all parts of the world which appears on the same day in
English papers, so that all round the world British people
are thinking of the same things at the same time. It is
calculated that more than one thousand pounds are spent

every day in paying for messages between Australia and Britain alone.

Thus we see that in many ways it is a mistake to think in these days that oceans divide, any more than land does.

British Citizenship.

Great numbers of people go away every year from the United Kingdom to find homes and employment for themselves in distant lands.

The same thing happens in other crowded European countries, such as Germany, Italy, Sweden, or Denmark. But one great difference between the case of emigrants from any of these countries and of those from our own must be noted. Those nations do not possess great territories abroad such as we have, and therefore, when a German, Italian, or Scandinavian emigrates from his native land, he has usually not only to give up his home, but also his nationality. He must become a citizen of a different State, live under a different flag, be governed by different laws, and change his old relations of life in many ways.

The Variety of the Empire.

With us it is quite different.

An inhabitant of the United Kingdom may go to countries which cover a large part of the world, and still be a British citizen—protected by the same flag—governed by the same laws—and, if he wish it, enjoying life in ways very similar to those to which he has been accustomed.

The choice which is open to anyone who wishes to leave these islands and still remain a British subject is very remarkable. If he desire to retain many of the customs of life with which he is familiar, and to live among people of his own race, he can do so in those temperate regions of the earth which we have settled in **Canada, New Zealand,** or **Australia.** If he prefer to seek an entire change of climate and to live among a strange race, he can do so in **India,** in parts of **Africa,** and in some of the tropical islands which belong to the **Empire.** Among our other possessions he may find almost every variety of climate and the most varied conditions of life.

He may go to regions where the people are employed chiefly in agricultural or pastoral pursuits. In these he may choose between places adapted for cultivating wheat or rice, tea or coffee, grapes or sugar-cane or tobacco—the fruits of the temperate zones or those of the tropics.

He can find large districts peculiarly fitted for rearing cattle and horses, or others where almost everyone is engaged in rearing sheep. He may choose parts of the Empire where people gain their living chiefly from the forests, or from fisheries, or from mines of gold, silver, tin, copper, or coal. He may find a home by the sea-coast or on wide prairies, in mountainous districts or beside great inland lakes and rivers.

Or, again, the emigrant may select some centre where new cities are rapidly growing up and where there is an opportunity for industry and skill of almost every kind.

But wherever he goes and whatever he does he will constantly be reminded that he has not lost his connection with this country. Not only will he still be under the same flag and governed for the most part by the same laws, but he will also find that in his business or industry he will still be closely bound up with the business and industry of the people of the United Kingdom.

The books which he reads, the clothes that he wears, the tools which he uses, will in many cases come from the Old Country, while he will send back in return the products of his industry—wool, cotton, wheat, sugar, beef, mutton, gold, silver, copper, and a thousand other articles which we at home require.

Round the Empire.

It is to see our British people in the homes which they have made abroad—to learn something about the countries which they have occupied, the work they do, their habits of life, the connection of their industry with ours, the many ways in which we are all bound together by common interests and duties, that we are now about to visit the distant parts of the Empire.

To do this we must make a tour all around the world. First, crossing the **Atlantic** to **America**, we shall there be able to study **Canada** and **Newfoundland** in the north, and further south **Bermuda**, the **West India Islands**, our two possessions of **British Guiana** and **British Honduras** on the adjoining mainland, and the islands which we have occupied off Cape Horn.

If from the western coast of Canada we cross the **Pacific Ocean**, we may observe the various groups of small islands which we possess over its vast surface, and then visit in the Southern Hemisphere the great colonies of **New Zealand, Australia** and **Tasmania**.

Crossing the Indian Ocean from Australia to **Africa,**
we shall see how our countrymen have already occupied the
southern part of that continent, have established important
posts and hold territory along the western and eastern
coasts, and at many points are gradually extending inland
the range of their influence.

Passing on to the continent of Asia, we shall there
have to study **India,** by far the greatest Dependency
ever ruled over by any European Power, and with
a population almost equal to that of the whole of
Europe.

Ceylon, parts of **Borneo** and **New Guinea,** and the
many islands and ports which are under our flag in the
Indian and China seas, must next be noted. It will then
remain for us to complete our tour by visiting those important positions which we have acquired, and in many
cases strongly fortified, in order to guard the two great
sea-routes by which the commerce of the East and of
Australasia chiefly comes to Europe—the one through the
Suez Canal and the **Mediterranean Sea,** the other around
the **Cape of Good Hope.**

Crossing the Ocean. Good bye.

Let us try to picture to ourselves a scene such as we
may observe almost any day in the week all the year
round if we go down to the docks of a great shipping
port like London, Liverpool, or Glasgow.

A great ocean steamboat is starting for Canada, Australia, South Africa, or the United States. For days
past gangs of men have been busy stowing away into

her vast hold merchandise of many kinds, chiefly goods
manufactured in the factories and workshops of Britain,
and selected to suit the wants of the country to which the
vessel is going.   Other gangs of men have been filling
her bunkers with hundreds of tons of coal, which will be
required as fuel for the engines that drive her across
the wide seas over which she must pass.   The heavy baggage of passengers, containing things they do not want
to use during the voyage, but which they will require in
the lands to which they go, is being stowed away in the
baggage-rooms below deck.   Hundreds of post-bags, full
of letters and papers, have been brought on board and
sent to the mail-room.

Passengers are coming on board, and mingled with
them on the decks and wharves are the crowds of friends
who have come to say farewell, or the spectators who are
always drawn together by the departure of an ocean
steamship.

Porters are busy carrying luggage, steam is up, and
the officers are at their posts.

All is ready at last—a bell rings—visitors hasten to
leave the ship; the gangways are drawn in; the cables
which fasten the vessel are loosed; the captain touches a
bell; down in the engine-room the huge pistons begin to
move; and then amid shouts of good-bye, the tears of those
sad at parting, the cheers of the light-hearted, and much
waving of hats and handkerchiefs, the great vessel glides
smoothly away on her long voyage.

Sometimes this scene is varied a little, when the steamship has to be anchored, as often happens at Liverpool, far

out in the river Mersey, and passengers are brought to her on a smaller steam-vessel or "tender" from the landing-stage.

The Mouth of the Mersey.

It is on a steamship thus leaving the Mersey that we are to cross the Atlantic and begin our tour of the British Empire. As we stand on the deck, let us begin at once to look around us. On our right is Liverpool, on our left the large town of **Birkenhead**. For miles on either side stretches the long line of docks and quays, crowded with vessels of every description. From what we see we can easily understand that Liverpool is one of the largest shipping ports in the world. No less than 23,000 vessels enter and leave the port in a single year. What is it that brings so many ships to Liverpool? It is not that the harbour itself is a very good one. On the contrary, the entrance to the Mersey is very difficult, and sometimes dangerous.

A bar of sand formed by the current and the tide lies across the entrance, and in foggy weather or at low tide ships cannot cross it. The bar itself is perpetually changing its position and its shape, and the Mersey pilots have to study its changes with the greatest care. Why then is Liverpool one of the greatest ports in the world? The reason is that behind it is the richest and most populous district in England with the exception of London. The cotton-mills of Lancashire alone make many millions of yards of cotton materials in the year, and every pound of the raw cotton required to supply the looms of Lancashire comes to the Mersey.

But where there are many mills there will be many workers, and the workers must be fed. English fields and pastures no longer furnish sufficient corn or cattle to supply their wants. Sometimes in a single year 20,000,000 quarters of wheat, and hundreds of thousands of cattle, are imported into Great Britain, and a large part of both come to Liverpool. Besides the live cattle, millions of pounds of meat are brought to the port. This does not nearly exhaust the list of commodities which are brought into the Mersey in enormous quantities for the use of the great manufacturing population of Lancashire, Yorkshire, and other parts of the North of England.

The ships which come to the Liverpool wharves with full cargoes leave them again as full. Cotton and woollen goods made in our mills, machinery from our iron-works, and hundreds of other articles manufactured in this country, are exported from Liverpool to all parts of the world. We should remember all these facts, for they teach us a lesson which we shall observe to be true in many other places as well as Liverpool. We shall find that a great harbour only becomes a great commercial port when it has at the back of it a wealthy and populous country, requiring the productions of other lands and seeking in them a market for what it has to sell.

Great ships pass us coming up the stream as we go down. Here are two steamers arriving at their destination at the same hour. One has come nearly 10,000 miles from the far East, bringing tea from **Hong Kong** in China. The other has made a voyage of about 8,500 miles from the **West Coast of South America,** and has

brought from Chili a cargo of nitrate to be used as manure
upon our English fields. We see many other ships coming
from different corners of the world, with cargoes of various
kinds. Others are setting out for distant ports.

The Flags of the Nations.

Notice the difference in the flags which they carry.
By an agreement between the Governments of all countries
every ship must carry some flag showing to what country
she belongs.

That large steamer coming up the river carries the red,
white, and black flag of Germany. The blue, white, and
red yonder is the famous French tricolour, on board a
steamer from Havre or Bordeaux; the red and yellow is a
Spaniard from Barcelona.

Inside the docks are many sailing-ships carrying large
bright flags made up of several crosses with a great deal of
red, yellow, and blue in them; these are timber-ships from
Sweden or Norway.

On the foremast of one great steamer fly the " stars
and stripes" of the United States, showing us that the
vessel has just arrived from New York. But there is
one flag which we see more often than all the others put
together: a bright red flag with the Union Jack in the
corner. It is the " red ensign," which I hope every
Englishman knows is the flag borne by all the merchant-
ships of the British Empire.

It is not wonderful, you will perhaps say, that in a
British port the British flag should be the most con-
spicuous. But sail the wide world round, follow every

pathway of the ocean, and enter every port where ships are to be found, and you will find our own red ensign on more than half the ships you see.

Outward Bound.

Now we have crossed the Mersey bar, and as night falls, the coast of England sinks out of sight behind us.

FIG. 2.—WHITE STAR STEAMER "MAJESTIC."
(From a Photograph by Medrington, 29, Bold Street, Liverpool.)

But we have not yet quite said good-bye to the United Kingdom. As we steer North-West we see on our left the coast of Ireland, on our right the coast of Scotland. The mouth of **Belfast Lough** opens to the West. A little further North and the lights on the **Mull of Cantire** in Scotland and **Fair Head** in Ireland show us that we are in that crowded channel by which ships pass into the Clyde and up to Glasgow. In the morning our vessel turns sharply from her direct course around the North of

Ireland, enters **Lough Foyle**, and comes to anchor at **Moville**, some miles below the famous town of **Derry**.

The Mails.

There is, of course, a special reason for this interruption to our voyage. Hours after we left Liverpool yesterday people in London and other large towns were writing letters or posting newspapers which our ship is to carry to Canada.

Sent off in the evening, the mails have been carried during the night by fast trains to Holyhead in Wales, thence by a swift packet-boat across St. George's Channel to Kingstown, and again hurried on by rail to catch us here. All this trouble is taken that we may carry with us the very latest news and the very latest messages of business men or friends. A tender is waiting to receive the mail-bags the moment they arrive at Moville and to bring them off to our ship. With the returning tender you can, if you wish, send a sixpenny telegram, which will go to any part of the United Kingdom, to let your friends know that you are thus far on your voyage safe and well.

As soon as the mails are on board the anchor is weighed, and, with full steam ahead, in a few hours we find ourselves out of sight of land upon the broad Atlantic.

Fellow Passengers.

Now that we are out at sea let us look around at our fellow passengers. Most of them are British like ourselves—either Canadians, who have come to this country for business or pleasure, and are now, after a short stay, returning to Canada, or else emigrants who are leaving the old country for the first time to try their fortunes on the banks of the St. Lawrence or in the great Canadian North-West.

A few others there are who cannot speak English, or who speak it but poorly. These are Swedes, or Danes, or Germans, hardy, honest, industrious men who are leaving their own land to find a home under the British flag. In Canada they will be welcome, and there they will soon learn the English tongue and become excellent British subjects.

That short, dark man is a Japanese, returning to Tokio to teach his quick-witted countrymen what he has learnt during a couple of years' stay in Europe. His home is in the far East, and yet he is now starting with us Westward. We shall see later on that he has chosen the shortest and easiest route by which to return.

But far the greater number of those with us are hard-working men and women of our own British race : English, Irish, and Scottish. Some have families of boys and girls with them, some not. Altogether there are several hundreds of emigrants on board.

Emigration.

It was said at the beginning of this chapter that vessels like the one we are on, leave British ports almost every day in the whole year for some distant part of the world. They carry away with them immense quantities of goods, but equally wonderful is the number of men, women, and children which they take out of the country.

It is surprising to learn how great the number is. In thirty-three years, from 1853 to 1886, more than six millions of people of British birth left these islands to find homes in distant lands. This stream of emigration still goes on. In 1888 the number which left was a little over 280,000 ; in 1890 it was 218,000 ; in 1902, 205,910. Thus the numbers for a single year are equal to the population of a great town like Portsmouth or Bradford.

Why People Emigrate.

It is worth while thinking why all this stream of people has kept pouring away from this country for so many years, and still keeps on going. It is easy to tell a good many of the chief reasons for it.

For a long time lists have been kept of the numbers which go every year. From studying these lists we find that when times are prosperous and labour plentiful the number of emigrants decreases, but when the crops have failed, or when times are bad and labour scarce, it increases rapidly. This shows you that a great many leave because they cannot find work in this crowded country, and so make up their minds to go to places where they think labourers are needed.

Some go in the hope of making a fortune quickly. These are often energetic men, who are doing very well in this country, and are not at all compelled to leave it. But they have heard of gold, or silver, or diamond mines, where men have made themselves rich by a few weeks or months of work, and they hope to do the same. Sometimes they succeed, but more commonly they are

c

disappointed. Still, though they do not get all they
want, they at least often find that they can make for
themselves comfortable and pleasant homes in the lands to
which they go.

Some go from a love of adventure. They have heard of
the rough life in the Australian bush, in Canadian forests,
or out on the prairies, of hunting, fishing, or explora-
tion in strange countries or among strange races, and,
discontented with a quiet life at home, they go abroad to
see new lands and have new experiences. All through our
history we may see how this spirit of roving and adventure
seems to have been in our British blood. It brought our
Saxon ancestors away from Germany across the North Sea
to explore and fight and find new homes, and later it sent
men like Drake, Raleigh, Cook, and Anson on strange
enterprises all around the world. Every year it sends
numbers of young Englishmen to climb the most difficult
mountain-peaks or hunt in lonely jungles, merely from a
desire to attempt something never accomplished before.
If a brave leader wishes to find a way to the North Pole,
or a bold explorer wants to penetrate into the heart of
Africa, he always finds plenty of volunteers ready to
follow him, though in the one case they are likely to
perish by cold, and in the other by the desert heat. This
love of adventure sometimes tempts people to try very
foolish things, but it has had a great deal to do with the
spread of our race over the world.

Often a man with a large family, even though he is
doing very well here, goes abroad to one of the Colonies
because he thinks that in a new country his children will

have a better chance than they would if they grew up here.
He breaks his ties with the old land, and starts life again
in a new one, for the sake of those who come after him.

Once more, there is always a great deal of money in
this country which the owners want to employ in business
enterprises. Rich men often find that it pays best to
use this in new or distant countries. So they send out
engineers and workmen to build railroads and construct
bridges, or open mines, and agents or clerks to direct their
business for them. Hundreds of millions of British money
are thus employed in distant parts of the world, and
thousands of Englishmen are employed abroad in its
management.

These are some of the chief causes which help to swell
the tide of emigration from our shores. But we must not fail
to notice that, while so many go away, population goes on
increasing rapidly at home. There are about four million
more people in the United Kingdom now than there were
ten years ago. We shall see after a while that the more
our people go abroad the more likely is there to be plenty
of work for those who stay at home, with abundant and
cheap food to support the workers.

Land ahead!—Newfoundland.

When we have been about five days at sea, the weather,
hitherto bright and warm, changes : the sky is overcast, and
a heavy fog lies on the water. A thermometer would show
us that the actual temperature of the sea-water has gone
down several degrees. The men on the look-out redouble
their watchfulness, for the fog may hide many dangers.

What is the meaning of this sudden change? It means that we are approaching the land, and are nearing the coast of **Newfoundland**. At this point a cold current meets us, coming from the Polar Sea, bringing with it great icebergs broken off from the masses of ice which everywhere surround the North Pole. East of the coast of Newfoundland this cold water meets a warm current which flows across the Atlantic from the Gulf of Mexico to the shores of Great Britain, and which is known as the **Gulf Stream**. The warm southern current has filled the atmosphere with moisture, which is condensed into vapour by the colder water of the north, and thus are created the dense fogs which so frequently hang around the island of Newfoundland.

Not only have the sailors to fear that in the fog the ship may come in collision with some other vessel, but there is the danger that at any moment the look-out may see, towering above, the white form of some gigantic iceberg.

The speed of the ship is reduced for greater safety, and a careful look-out enables us to avoid all perils.

Soon we begin to see numbers of sailing-boats rocking upon the waves. These are the boats of the cod-fishers, of whom we shall learn more when we come to speak of Newfoundland. At present our steamship is bound further west.

The Short Cut across the Atlantic.

In the summer months a steamship going from Great Britain to Canada has the choice of two routes—one by the north of Newfoundland through the **Straits of Belleisle**, which gives the shortest passage to **Quebec** or **Montreal**; the other **south of Newfoundland**, which is always used for reaching the ports of **Halifax** or **St. John**, and for entering the **St. Lawrence** also when there is danger of delay from meeting ice by the northern route.

As we are now nearly across the Atlantic, it is well to note one or two points with regard to the routes by which

FIG. 3.— STEAMER ROUTES ACROSS THE ATLANTIC.

that ocean may be crossed. From **Liverpool** to **Halifax** is **2,680** miles, from **Liverpool** to **Quebec** by the Straits of Belleisle is **2,693** miles; but from **Liverpool** to **New York** in the United States is **3,025** miles. Subtract 2,680 from 3,025, and we shall see how much further it is to the chief port of the United States than to the British port of Halifax. Now a glance at the map shows that New York is a good deal further from Liverpool than Halifax, and a

little further than Quebec.   But from the map we cannot
well understand how great the difference is, and we must look
at the globe before we can do so. The lines which circle
the globe and are known as parallels of latitude grow longer
and longer as they get near to the centre line or Equator.

The further north the shorter the distance around the
globe. Halifax is many miles north of New York, and
Quebec still further.   A ship, therefore, sailing from
Liverpool to Quebec or Halifax moves along a smaller
circle than when sailing to New York. As both of the
Canadian ports are also east of New York, you can now
understand why Halifax has an advantage of 345 miles,
and Quebec of 332 miles, over New York in the length of
the passage between them and Liverpool. This is almost as
far as a good steamship can go in a day. Canadian ports,
therefore, give a route between Europe and America con-
siderably shorter than harbours further south.

The St. Lawrence.

Our vessel is to go by the shorter voyage to Halifax, as
we wish to cross Canada from East to West. The traveller,
however, who in summer goes by the more northern
passage finds it the grandest and most impressive of all
the approaches to the American continent. As he enters
the Straits of Belleisle he can reflect that from this point
to the head of **Lake Superior**, at the heart of the continent,
2,384 miles distant, is an unbroken system of navigation
by gulf, river, lake, or canal.

Passing through the narrow passage which separates
the rock-bound coasts of Labrador from those of New

foundland, he finds himself in the Gulf of St. Lawrence, the land-locked sea which is the chief centre of Canada's vast fishing industries. Sailing westward past the large island of **Anticosti**, he enters the mouth of the **St. Lawrence**, one of the greatest rivers of the world—the outlet for lakes which contain nearly one-half of all the fresh water on the globe. As the river narrows so that its banks may be seen, he finds them settled by a population gradually growing denser as he ascends the stream.

The river itself is seen to be already one of the important routes of the world's commerce. Sailing-vessels laden with timber or wheat; steamships carrying live cattle, or cargoes of meat, cheese, flour, fruit, or other provisions, pass constantly on their way to Britain, while others from Europe are ascending the stream. Further up, the scenery grows more striking and beautiful, till at last the traveller comes in sight of that which so stirred the enthusiasm of the first explorers of the country—the noble promontory on which are situated the historic city and citadel of **Quebec**.

The Southern Route.

But we must go back to the less magnificent, though scarcely less interesting, approach to the coast of Nova Scotia, the most eastern Province of Canada. Escaping from the fogs of Newfoundland, we steam towards the harbour of **Halifax**. We see that the channel through which we enter is narrow enough to be well defended by the fortifications armed with powerful batteries by which we pass. To the left, along the sides of the harbour, rises the city, crowned by the citadel, high over which

floats the British flag. Ahead of us, stretching inland
for some miles, is Bedford Basin, a splendid sheet of
water in which the whole navy of Britain could easily
be anchored. A part of it is there as we enter, for
Halifax is the chief station for the British North

FIG. 4. — BRITISH MEN-OF-WAR IN HALIFAX HARBOUR.

American squadron. As our steamship comes up to her
pier, we see that it is crowded with people—some waiting
to meet friends, others drawn together by mere curiosity.
British soldiers and British sailors, in their familiar uniforms, are mingled among the crowd.

New Friends under Old Names.

The emigrants on board who are watching everything
closely may see that the new land to which they have

come is very like the old land
they have left. The looks of
the people, their dress, their
language, their manners, are
the same. We learn the same
thing as we walk along the
streets from the names over
the shop doors—Smith, Brown,
Robinson ; O'Brien, O'Donnell,
Daley ; McDonald, Fraser,
McGregor—here are English,
Irish and Scottish names repeated over and over again.

Here, again, is an English
Church, and there a Presby-
terian ; Methodist, Baptist, or
Roman Catholic places of wor-
ship are not far off. So it is,
we shall find, over a large part
of our widespread British world.

From Ocean to Ocean by Rail.

The last thing we took
on board at Moville was the
mails ; they are the first to be
landed at Halifax. At the
railway station, not far off, a
special train is waiting to
receive them. Soon they are

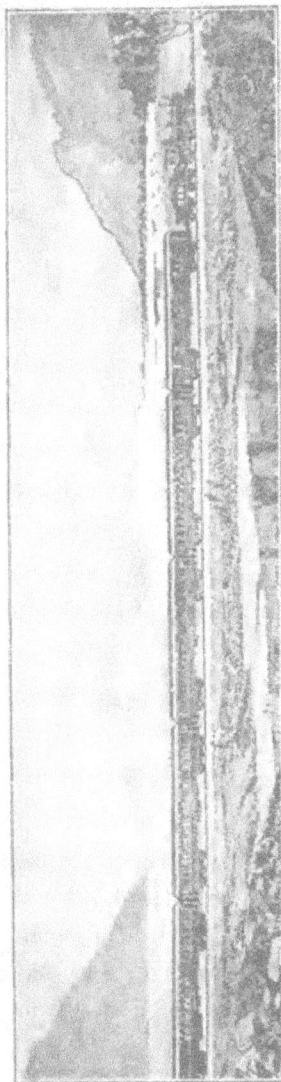

FIG. 4 CANADIAN PACIFIC TRAIN PASSING SCHUSWAP LAKE, BRITISH COLUMBIA.

all on board, together with such passengers as have been
ready to transfer themselves with their baggage at once
from the steamship.

The train starts off. That line of rails over which it
moves stretches away to the westward without a single

FIG. 6.—THE SNOW-PLOUGH AT WORK.

break for more than 3,500 miles. It runs by thousands
of fertile farms, through cities and villages, through
gloomy forests—over wide, rushing rivers spanned by some
of the largest bridges in the world, across prairies which
seem to have no end—along the edge of precipices—over
the summits of lofty mountains, and then down again
through sunny valleys till it has reached the waters of the
Pacific. All this time it has been on British soil. At

each of the cities where the train stops it leaves some of the mail-bags taken on board at Liverpool and Moville. The letters and newspapers which they contain are soon distributed all over the country, and not only through Canadian cities and villages, but also in the loneliest farmhouses on the prairie or in the forest, the messages and news from home are being read.*

By spending a few shillings on a cable message, a passenger can, when he reaches Halifax, let his friends at home know in a few minutes that his ocean voyage is safely over. Even if he does not do this, they may easily find out, if they choose, about the arrival of his ship. Every morning many of the chief papers in the United Kingdom publish lists which show what British vessels have arrived, on the day before, at the principal ports in all parts of the world. This intelligence is collected by the newspapers because so many of the people who read them are interested in knowing about the coming and going of the ships which carry mails, passengers, or merchandise.

* Separate trains are usually provided for the emigrants who are going westward to the remoter parts of Canada. These trains are specially prepared for the comfort of travellers during a journey of several days and nights. At night the cars are furnished with sleeping-berths, and during the day " kitchen cars " are attached to each train, so that meals can be cooked and eaten while the journey is going on. An emigrant can now be transferred from Great Britain to the prairies of North-Western Canada in eleven or twelve days, and with very little fatigue.

FIG. 7.—THE BEAVER AND THE MAPLE-LEAF.

CHAPTER II.

THE GREAT DOMINION.

The Size of Canada.

THIS great country to which we have come is the Dominion of Canada. Stretching East and West from the Atlantic to the Pacific, about 3,500 miles, and from the Gulf of St. Lawrence and the Great Lakes northward to the Polar Sea; with an area of about **three and a half millions of square miles**, or nearly as great as the whole of Europe; it is the largest state of the British Empire. With more than **five millions of inhabitants** already, it has room within its wide borders for many millions more. If, when we have crossed the Atlantic, we were to land at Halifax or St. John, the most Eastern ports, we should find that at least six days and nights of steady travelling by an express train, including necessary stoppages, would be required to carry us from one side of Canada to the other. This fact may help us to understand how vast the country is.

How Canada became a Part of the Empire.

But before we say more about this great country, it is well that we should learn how it became a part of the British

FIG. 8.—QUEBEC, FROM THE ST. LAWRENCE.

Empire. That it should ever do so seemed very unlikely for more than two centuries after its discovery. The early settlers were French, and the Government of France exerted itself greatly to build up here a powerful French community. This it succeeded in doing, and yet the people are now British citizens and the country a part of the Empire. That we may understand how this came about let us visit the famous city of **Quebec**. Why do we say

FIG. 9.—MONUMENT TO GENERAL WOLFE.

the *famous* city of Quebec? The reason is found in its history.

If we approach Quebec by the river the frowning citadel towers high above us. Disembarking, we walk through streets which remind the traveller at every step of the old French towns of Normandy or Brittany. Climbing a steep

path, we pass through an archway which was the ancient
entrance to the fortress, and furnished with massive gates.
Going up still higher, we reach the terrace of the citadel.
Men have said, after travelling all round the world, that they
had seen no nobler view than that which meets the eye from
this terrace as one looks down upon the broad St. Lawrence,
the cliffs of **Point Levis** opposite, the fertile island of Orleans
below, and the blue Laurentian hills in the distance. But
we must look further than this noble view to find that which
makes Quebec most famous. We leave the city by another
gate, and at some distance on the open plain see a lofty
monument of stone. Upon it is the simple inscription :

> HERE DIED
> WOLFE
> VICTORIOUS,
> SEP. XII.
> MDCCLIX.

The battle on the **Plains of Abraham,** in which General
Wolfe fell, was one of the turning-points in the world's
history. Canada, hitherto colonised and governed by
France, now became a part of the British Empire. The
French people of the Province of Quebec became British
subjects, and what had before been doubtful was now
settled, namely, that people of British stock, rather than
French, should control the greater part of the North
American Continent. We can now understand what
people are thinking of when they speak of Quebec as a
very famous city.

How Canada has been Kept for the Empire.

We have seen how Canada was taken from France.
Let me now say something about how it has been kept for

Britain. Not many years after Wolfe's great victory at Quebec, the war of the American Revolution broke out. The English colonies south of Canada revolted from the Mother Country, and established an independent Government of their own under the name of the United States. Wishing to conquer Canada, they made an attack upon Quebec, but were defeated, and their general was slain, in an attempt to capture the citadel. Already the French people of the Province had become so satisfied with British rule that they assisted in repelling the invaders.

The "Loyalists."

Soon after this, Canada received a large body of settlers who had a great influence on the future history of the country. When the war of the American Revolution was over, there were still in the United States a considerable number of people who had throughout continued loyal to the British Government. Unwilling to remain as citizens of the new Republic, and in some cases suffering persecution there, great numbers of them removed to Canada. They have always been known and honoured as the **United Empire Loyalists.** These Loyalists, to the number of about 40,000, found homes in the Provinces of Ontario, Nova Scotia, and New Brunswick, districts then covered almost entirely with forest, but which soon became filled by their labours with pleasant farms and prosperous villages and towns. It was not long, however, before they were called upon to defend the homes they had thus created and the flag which they had sacrificed and suffered so much to live under.

In 1812 war again broke out between Britain and the United States, and the people of the latter country again undertook the conquest of Canada. Although the whole population of Canada was then but 300,000, against 8,000,000 of their hostile neighbours, the country boldly prepared to meet the coming danger. Loyalists and French Canadians fought with equal bravery beside the few regulars of the British army then stationed in Canada.

Their efforts were crowned with success; the troops of the United States were driven back at almost every point of attack, and when the war closed in 1815, though many valuable lives had been lost, no inch of soil was surrendered, and Canada has since been left free to develop herself as a part of the British Empire. In this way the Canadian people have proved their right to be considered among the most patriotic of British citizens.

Self-Government for the Colonies.

But Canadians had to learn to govern their country as well as defend it. When the different provinces were first settled or taken possession of, governors, judges, and other officers were sent out from England to manage their affairs, and make and administer their laws. Now it is a characteristic of our British people when they go abroad, just as it is at home, that they desire, so far as it is possible and wise, to govern themselves. This does not mean that every man wishes to do as he pleases, for good government is not possible in that way. It means that he wishes to have a voice in making the laws by which he is governed.

D

As the new provinces increased in population, they soon began to feel that they could make their own local laws better than anyone else, and that they ought to be allowed to tax themselves and spend as they pleased the money raised by taxation. After a great deal of discussion, Parliament agreed to this claim that the people of Canada had as much right to control their taxation and like matters as the people of Great Britain and Ireland have in the United Kingdom, and so each province was allowed to form a **Legislature** or small Parliament of its own, while it had a governor, not to make laws, but to represent the Sovereign, and to occupy in these Provincial Parliaments the same position as the King occupies in the Imperial Parliament.

In this way the Canadian provinces secured the right of self-government under the Crown. This was a very important step, since it has done more than anything else to keep Canadians as contented and happy as are subjects of the Empire in Britain itself. You will find that in all the great colonies where the inhabitants are chiefly of British or European descent this same plan of leaving the people to govern themselves is followed. Where the people of a colony are chiefly of other races this cannot be done, but even in that case our object is to give as large a measure of self-government as possible to those who are under our rule.

Canadian Confederation.

For many years after they were allowed to govern themselves the provinces of Canada remained independent

of each other, each managing its own affairs in its own
way. But in the year 1867 a great and important
change was made.

The leading public men of the country met together,
and planned a system by which all the provinces should be
united under one Government, with one great Parliament
to manage affairs in which the whole country was interested,
while each province kept its smaller Legislature to attend
to what only concerned itself.

This Union was called **The Canadian Confederation.**
The Provinces united in this way then received in 1867
the name of "**The Dominion of Canada,**" and **Ottawa** was
selected as the seat of Government. Since that time,
instead of a governor for each province, only one Governor-
General goes out from Great Britain to represent the
King, as the head of the Government in the Dominion.

At the head of this chapter we see a representation of
the **Beaver** at work surrounded by a border composed of
the beautiful **Maple Leaf.** The **Beaver** and the **Maple Leaf**
have been chosen by the Canadians as national emblems
of the industry and wealth of their land. The beaver
always working busily among the timber by the water-side
in the great rivers is a fit emblem of the great "lumbering" and river industries of Canada, while the maple leaf,
gathered from the sugar maple, recalls the great agricultural riches of a country of corn and of apples.

CHAPTER III.

THE PHYSICAL FEATURES OF CANADA.

WE have now learned how Canada became a part of the British Empire, and why it has remained so. Let us consider some of the more striking features of the country.

Observe that on the East there is a great extent of sea-coast, with many bays, gulfs, and inlets, chief among which are the **Gulf of St. Lawrence**, the **Bay of Fundy**, and **Chaleur Bay**, while further North is **Hudson Bay**, an inland sea 1,000 miles long and 600 miles broad.

On the Western side of the continent, again, we find a long stretch of sea-coast much broken up by bays, sounds, and inlets, which offer remarkable opportunities for navigation and commerce.

Thus Canada has a most striking maritime position on two great oceans, the Atlantic, which lies between it and Europe, and the Pacific, which separates it from Asia.

The **fisheries** on the Eastern and Western coasts are probably the most valuable and extensive in the world, and give employment to a large seafaring population.

Excellent timber is obtained with the greatest ease close to the sea-coast, and consequently great encouragement has been given to ship-building.

The people build and own great numbers of ships, which are engaged in the fisheries, the coasting trade, and that of the inland lakes, or in carrying on commerce with distant parts of the world. As a result of all these circumstances the Dominion stands third in the number

of its merchant vessels and fourth in tonnage among all
the nations of the world

Thus the maritime situation and industries of the

FIG. 10.—A STREET
SCENE IN CANADA
—WINTER.

country have given Canada, just as they have given
Britain, many interests upon the ocean.

The Waterways of the Dominion.

The feature of the Dominion which next deserves notice
is its wonderful system of inland water communication.

We have before spoken of the immense extent of the, country. Wide as it is, however, it is curiously open in almost every part to the traveller, the trader, or the settler. The most characteristic feature of Canada is the remarkable number and size of its rivers. In connection with the great lakes which have been mentioned, and other smaller ones, these rivers stretch across the whole breadth of the continent, and furnish it with an almost unbroken series of water highways such as no other country in the world possesses.

When the **Marquis of Dufferin** was Governor-General of Canada he described this wonderful system of waterways in a witty speech which he made at the city of Winnipeg in Manitoba.

We shall quote a part of his graphic description. After mentioning that the small size of the maps on which the figure of the world is depicted had prevented even educated people from forming an adequate idea of the extent of the British posséssions in North America, he said :—

A Wonderful Picture.

" Perhaps the best way of correcting such a misapprehension would be a summary of the rivers which flow through them, for we know that, as a poor man cannot live in a big house, so a small country cannot support a big river.

" Now to an Englishman or a Frenchman the Severn or the Thames, the Seine or the Rhone, would appear considerable streams ; but in the **Ottawa**, a mere affluent of the **St. Lawrence**, an affluent, moreover, which reaches the parent stream six hundred miles from its mouth, we have

FIG. 11.—LAKE OF THE WOODS.

a river nearly five hundred and fifty miles long, and three .
or four times as big as any of them.

"But even after having ascended the St. Lawrence itself
to Lake Ontario, and pursued it across **Lake Erie, St. Clair,
Lake Huron,** and **Lake Superior** to **Thunder Bay**—a
distance of fifteen hundred miles, where are we? In the
estimation of a person who has made the journey, at the
end of all things ; but to us, who know better, scarcely at
the beginning of the great fluvial systems of the Dominion ;
for from that spot, that is to say, from Thunder Bay, we
are able at once to ship our astonished traveller on to the
Kaministiquia, a river of some hundred miles long. Thence,
almost in a straight line, we launch him on to **Lake
Shebandowan,** and **Rainy Lake and River**—a magnificent
stream three hundred yards broad and a couple of hundred
miles long, down whose tranquil bosom he floats to the **Lake
of the Woods,** where he finds himself on a sheet of water
which, though diminutive as compared with the inland
seas he has left behind him, will probably be found
sufficiently extensive to render him fearfully sea-sick during
his passage across it.

"For the last eighty miles of his voyage, however, he
will be consoled by sailing through a succession of land-
locked channels, the beauty of whose scenery, while it
resembles, certainly excels the far-famed Thousand Islands
of the St. Lawrence.

"From this lacustrine paradise of sylvan beauty we are
able at once to transfer our friend to the **Winnipeg,** a
river whose existence in the very heart and centre of
the continent is in itself one of Nature's most delightful

miracles—so beautiful and varied are its rocky banks,
its tufted islands; so broad, so deep, so fervid is the
volume of its waters, the extent of their lake-like ex-
pansions, and the tremendous power of their rapids.

" At last let us suppose we have landed our traveller at
the town of Winnipeg, the half-way house of the continent, the capital of the Prairie Province. . . . Having
had so much of water, having now reached the home of
the buffalo, like the extenuated Falstaff he naturally
"babbles of green fields" and careers in imagination over
the green grasses of the prairie. Not at all. . . . We
take him down to your quay and ask him which he will
ascend first—the **Red River** or the **Assiniboine**—two
streams, the one five hundred miles long, the other four
hundred and eighty, which so happily mingle their waters
within your city limits. After having given him a
preliminary canter up these respective rivers we take him
off to **Lake Winnipeg**, an inland sea 300 miles long and
upwards of 60 broad, during the navigation of which, for
many a weary hour, he will find himself out of sight of
land, and probably a good deal more indisposed than ever
he was on the Lake of the Woods, or even the Atlantic.

"At the north-west angle of Lake Winnipeg he hits
upon the mouth of the **Saskatchewan**, the gateway to the
North-West, and the starting point to another 1,500 miles
of navigable water flowing nearly due East and West
between its alluvial banks.

" Having now reached the foot of the **Rocky Mountains**,
our Ancient Mariner—for by this time he will be quite
eatitled to such an appellation—knowing that water cannot

run up-hill, feels certain his aquatic experiences are concluded.

"He was never more mistaken. We immediately launch him upon the **Athabasca** and **Mackenzie Rivers,** and start him on a longer trip than he has yet undertaken—the navigation of the Mackenzie River alone exceeding 2,500 miles. If he survives this last experience we wind up his peregrinations by a concluding voyage of 1,400 miles down the **Fraser River,** or, if he prefers it, the **Thompson River,** to Victoria, in Vancouver, whence, having previously provided him with a first-class return ticket for that purpose, he will probably prefer getting home *riá* the **Canadian Pacific.**

"Now, in this enumeration, those who are acquainted with the country are aware that, for the sake of brevity, I have omitted thousands of miles of other lakes and rivers which water various regions of the North-West:—the **Qu'Appelle River,** the **Belly River, Lake Manitoba, Lake Winnipegosis, Shoal Lake,** and others, along whose interminable banks and shores I might have dragged, and finally exterminated, our way-worn guest." *

Natural Divisions.

The vast breadth of Canada, which is watered by this remarkable system of lakes and rivers, may be roughly divided into four sections, each with a special character of its own.

1. The great Woodland Region, extending over the

---

* A larger map than can be given in this book may be used with advantage in tracing out the course of Earl Dufferin's imaginary journey.

South and East, and stretching from the Atlantic to the
head of the great lakes at the western extremity of
Ontario.

2. The great PRAIRIE COUNTRY, beginning with the
Province of Manitoba, and extending westward to the foot
of the Rocky Mountains, with a varying breadth from north
to south of some hundreds of miles.

3. The MOUNTAIN REGION, which includes all between
the Rocky Mountains and the Pacific Ocean.

4. The ARCTIC SLOPE of the continent, extending from
the divisions already mentioned northward to the Frozen
Ocean.

The Climate of Canada.

When Louis the Fifteenth of France was signing the
treaty by which he gave up Canada to be a part of the
British Empire, he is said to have exclaimed, " After all,
it is only a few acres of snow." No doubt he said this to
make the loss of France and the gain of England seem less
than they were. But he also expressed an opinion which
was once very common about Canada. It was believed
that the cold was so severe and the snow lay so long upon
the ground that the country was scarcely fit for men to
live in. We now know that this was a mistake, and that
the climate of large parts of Canada is well suited for
Europeans, and particularly adapted for making the people
of the country healthy and hardy.

As Canada stretches from about the latitude of **Naples**
in Italy to the ocean which surrounds the North Pole, and
as it has lofty mountain ranges as well as level plains, the
differences of climate are great. Speaking generally of

the provinces which have been settled, it may be said that the winters are cold and the summers hot. All travellers agree, however, that the exceeding dryness of the atmosphere makes both cold and heat less felt than in countries where the air is moist.

In the Eastern or Maritime Provinces the winter climate is made less severe and the summer climate peculiarly delightful from the nearness of the sea. In Southern Ontario, peaches, grapes, and like fruits ripen freely in the open air, and are largely cultivated. On the far western prairies, in the territories near the Rocky Mountains, cattle are found to be sleek and fat after grazing outdoors through the winter months. Here the warm "Chinook" winds prevent the snow from lying long on the ground.

West of the Rocky Mountains, on the Pacific slope of British Columbia, the climate is milder than in any other part of Canada, and is considered one of the most delightful in the world.

The Canadian Winter.

To keep their homes comfortable in winter, Canadians build warm houses and have plentiful supplies of wood and coal. But while they do this, they live much in the open air. The singular clearness, dryness, and stillness of the atmosphere give to healthy people a feeling of exhilaration, so that winter is in Canada the favourite season for outdoor amusements. Canadian boys and girls love during the winter months to spend the whole day or the bright moonlight evenings in the clear cold air, keeping themselves warm with the brisk exercise of skating, snow-shoeing, tobogganning, or similar winter amusements, which they think more delightful than any others in the world.

The winters are long and the springs later than in England, but the warmth of summer makes the growth of vegetation so rapid that by the middle of July crops are as forward as in this country, and in some parts harvesting begins earlier than in the United Kingdom.

If we leave the settled provinces and go northward, the climate becomes colder and the winters longer. At last we reach a region unsuited for agriculture. Here the country is at first heavily wooded, but finally even the forest trees become stunted or altogether disappear.

♦♦♦

CHAPTER IV.

THE PROVINCES OF CANADA AND THEIR PRODUCTS.

Political Divisions.

THE Dominion is made up of seven Provinces—**Nova Scotia, Prince Edward Island, New Brunswick, Quebec, Ontario, Manitoba,** and **British Columbia,** with a vast region usually spoken of as the **North-West Territories,** out of which, as the country becomes settled, new provinces will be formed. This region has for the present been divided into large districts, the chief of which are **Alberta, Assiniboia, Saskatchewan,** and **Athabasca.**

The capital city of the whole Dominion is **Ottawa,** situated on the Ottawa River, and in the Province of Ontario. Here are the Parliament Buildings and the great public offices, and here the Governor-General resides.

FIG. 12.—PARLIAMENT HOUSE, OTTAWA.

Ottawa is the centre of a large lumber trade. The Parliament Buildings occupy a very commanding site on the high banks of the Ottawa River.

We may now make a very brief study of each of the provinces into which Canada is divided.

The Maritime Provinces.

Under the rule of the French the present provinces of **Nova Scotia** and **New Brunswick** were known by the name of **Acadia**. Together with **Prince Edward Island,** they are now usually spoken of as the **Maritime Provinces** of Canada, from their position on the seaboard of the Dominion. The waters which surround them are the centre of the most important fisheries of Canada, which furnish employment to a considerable part of the population settled along the coasts. The harbours of the Maritime Provinces are of great importance to the commerce of Canada, since they are the only ones open throughout the year—those of the river St. Lawrence being closed by ice during the winter.

The Dominion has good winter ports at **Halifax, St. John,** and **St. Andrews.**

While the three Maritime Provinces are alike in having great fishing interests, their resources in other ways are different, and it will therefore be well to say something about them separately.

Nova Scotia.

Nova Scotia and the neighbouring island of Cape Breton, which forms part of the Province, have large deposits of excellent **coal,** of which we shall have occasion to speak more particularly in another chapter. **Iron-ore**. is found in great abundance and of excellent quality, and, as in England, the beds of iron-ore are near those of coal. **Gold** occurs over a considerable area of country, chiefly in veins of quartz, from which it is obtained by crushing.

Some districts of Nova Scotia are rocky and barren, but in others the soil is very fertile, suited for all kinds of agriculture, and peculiarly adapted for growing fruit. The orchards of Nova Scotia have long been famous, and there is a large export of **apples** to the markets of Britain and the United States.

The mines, farms, forests, and fisheries of Nova Scotia give its inhabitants a great variety of profitable occupation.

The chief city, **Halifax**, has one of the finest harbours in the Empire. It is strongly fortified, and is the only place in Canada where regiments of the Imperial army are still regularly stationed.

Halifax is also the summer station for our men-of-war of the North American squadron, and is the port to which Canadian mail-steamers come in the winter when the St. Lawrence is closed with ice.

Louisburg in Cape Breton and **Annapolis** on the Bay of Fundy are noted as having been old French strongholds.

New Brunswick.

New Brunswick was at one time the most densely wooded province of Canada, and it still has extensive forests in the centre and north of the country. Noble rivers flow eastward into the Gulf of St Lawrence and southward into the Bay of Fundy, and in every part the province is well watered. The scenery of the largest river, the St. John, is often compared in point of beauty with that of the Hudson or the Rhine.

For many years in its earlier history the industry of the people of New Brunswick was largely turned to the trade in timber and to ship-building. As the vast forests have been cleared away fertile farms have taken their place, and now along the valleys of the great rivers and in many other sections the country is filled with a prosperous agricultural population. There are still large areas of fertile forest-lands unoccupied and awaiting settlement, especially in the northern counties. The many railways which have been built in every direction through the province now make these lands easily accessible to the settler, and also furnish him with a ready means of sending his produce to market.

Some of the rivers of New Brunswick are widely known as salmon-fishing streams, and sportsmen come from many distant parts of the world every year to spend a few weeks upon their banks. The coasts of the Gulf of St. Lawrence and the Bay of Fundy attract in summer numbers of visitors who seek in the cool sea-breezes an escape from the severe heat of the inland and southern parts of America.

On the sea-coast of New Brunswick the people often combine the occupations of farmer and fisherman, in the inland parts of farmer and lumberman. Of the latter occupation we shall learn more further on.

E

St. John, the largest city, has a fine harbour, which is one of the winter ports of Canada. The capital of the province is **Fredericton**, beautifully situated on the banks

FIG. 13.—FREDERICTON CATHEDRAL.

of the St. John River, here more than half a mile wide. For weeks during the spring and early summer the surface of this broad river is covered with timber floating down towards the sea. It is on its way to England.

On the opposite page is a picture of the Cathedral at Fredericton. An English emigrant might imagine that it had been transplanted from his native village. It was, in truth, built to resemble the village church at Snettisham in Norfolk.

The Bay of Fundy.

The **Bay of Fundy**, which separates Nova Scotia from New Brunswick, has long been famed for having the highest tides in the world. They are supposed to be caused partly by the meeting of the tidal waves of the North and South Atlantic off the American coast, and partly by the peculiar shape of the Bay, which tapers gradually like a funnel, so that at its head the waters are compressed into a narrow space, and at flood-tides rise to the height of fifty or even sixty feet. The sediment deposited by these tides forms marshes

FIG. 11.—MAP OF CHIGNECTO SHIP RAILWAY.

of great extent. With immense labour large tracts have been protected from the inroads of the sea by means of dykes, but the exceeding fertility of the land well repays all the trouble which has been taken in reclaiming it. On

these marshes in both New Brunswick and Nova Scotia many cattle are reared and fattened for English markets.

A Ship Railway.

Looking at the small map of the Maritime Provinces on the preceding page, we see that the Province of Nova

FIG. 15.—AN "OVERLAND ROUTE."

Scotia is joined to New Brunswick by an isthmus or narrow neck of land. This isthmus, which is only eighteen miles wide, separates the waters of the Gulf of St. Lawrence from those of the Bay of Fundy. In passing from one to the other, ships have hitherto had to sail

several hundreds of miles round Nova Scotia. Owing to the
high tides which have been mentioned, and other reasons,
it was difficult to make a canal through the **Isthmus of
Chignecto**, and so clever engineers are constructing a
railway on which ships, either loaded or unloaded, can be
lifted, carried across the country, and deposited again in
the water on the other side of the isthmus. In commerce
we save expense when we shorten time and distance
between places. As in England tunnels have been cut
under broad rivers like the Thames, Severn, and Mersey
to make a saving of time and distance in railway travel,
so in Canada we have the Ship Railway used to save time
and distance for ships. On the opposite page is a picture
which illustrates the new method by which Canadians pro-
pose to shorten navigation around their coasts. Engineers
believe that the successful operation of a Ship Railway at
Chignecto will lead to its adoption in other places.

Prince Edward Island.

The little Province of **Prince Edward Island**, in the
Gulf of St. Lawrence, is often called the "Garden of
Canada." The soil is singularly fertile and highly cultivated, so that the scenery in much of the island strongly
resembles that of the best agricultural counties of England.
The attention of the people is almost entirely given up to
the two industries of fishing and farming. Oysters and
lobsters are exported in great quantities. In summer
the island is a favourite resort of tourists. In winter communication with the mainland is difficult, but is maintained
by means of vessels specially constructed to push a way

through the floating ice which then fills the neighbouring gulf and straits. It is proposed to get rid of this difficulty by constructing a tunnel under the straits to the nearest point of Nova Scotia.

Charlottetown is the capital and chief city of the province.

The Acadians.

In all the Maritime Provinces of Canada there are districts inhabited chiefly by the descendants of the early French settlers of the country, who are called **Acadians**. They commonly speak both French and English, and are a simple-minded, industrious peasantry, little changed from what they were more than a hundred years ago, when they first became British subjects.

Quebec and the French Canadians.

The Province of Quebec is nearly four times the size of England. When French Canadians first became British subjects in 1759 they only numbered between sixty and seventy thousand, but they have now increased to nearly a million and a half, and the great majority of these are found in the Province of Quebec. They have retained the French language and many French laws and customs, so that it is very difficult for a traveller to believe, in many parts of Quebec, that he is really in a British country. But there are few more contented and patriotic citizens of the Empire than the French Canadians, for they know that under the British Government they have obtained far more liberty than they ever had under that of France, and are free not only to govern themselves, but to take a large share in the government of the whole Dominion. The *habitants*, as the Quebec peasants are called, are, like the Acadians of the Maritime Provinces, a simple, contented, industrious people, much attached to the Roman Catholic

FIG. 16.—A " HABITANT."

religion and to the old customs which their ancestors brought from Normandy and Brittany. Among the better-educated classes English is spoken as freely as French, and some of the most brilliant speakers in the Canadian Parliament are Frenchmen who can be eloquent in both languages.

The River St. Lawrence flows through the Province of Quebec, and is the great outlet for the productions of the West. Down its many large tributaries are brought the vast quantities of timber which Quebec every year sends to Britain. ꞏSituated on the banks of the St. Lawrence are the two cities of **Quebec** and **Montreal**. The former was the ancient capital of French Canada, and still retains the massive walls which once made it an almost impregnable fortress.

Montreal is the largest city of the Dominion, and the centre of steam communication and trade with Great Britain. It is the Liverpool of Canada. All through the season when navigation is open, the long line of wharves along the St. Lawrence is crowded with steamships and sailing vessels, some unloading the cargoes of goods which they have brought, chiefly from Britain, others being laden with what Canada has to send back in return. In a single year there thus went away from Montreal about 6,000,000 bushels of grain, 100,000,000 lbs. of cheese, 60,000 head of cattle, 46,000 sheep, 270,000 barrels of apples, and 120,000,000 feet of lumber. From some of these figures we may learn how Canada helps to feed England.

Ontario.

Ontario is the wealthiest and most populous province of the Dominion. It has an area of more than 290,000 square miles, or 80,000 more than the whole of the United Kingdom. An unusually large proportion of the soil is fit for tillage, and much of it is exceedingly fertile. The great wealth of the country is in its farms, which

have been formed by gradually clearing away the forest.
Wheat, cattle, cheese, butter, and **fruit** are exported in
great quantities, chiefly to the United Kingdom. **Barley**
and some other forms of farm produce find a large market
in the United States.

Wide areas of unoccupied forest-land still exist, which
furnish **timber** for the British markets and offer homes to
the emigrant.

North of Lake Superior there is a wide extent of
country so rough and rocky that little of it is adapted to
agriculture. But this district is wonderfully rich in
minerals—especially **silver, copper, iron,** and **nickel,** the
last a metal which is becoming of great importance in the
arts, and is here found in greater abundance than in any
other part of the world. In the district bordering upon
Lake Huron rich **petroleum** wells and valuable **salt springs**
are found. Important manufacturing industries are
rapidly growing up in many of the cities and towns.

Bordered by the four great lakes, **Ontario, Erie, Huron,**
and **Superior,** and with the St. Lawrence furnishing an
outlet to the sea, Ontario is admirably situated for
carrying on trade with Britain, the United States, and the
other provinces of Canada.

The famous **Falls of Niagara** are upon a river of the
same name which separates Ontario from the State of
New York and connects Lake Erie with Lake Ontario.
Here the waters of the Great Lakes pour in a mighty
torrent over a precipice 158 feet high, presenting one of
the most magnificent sights to be met with in the whole
world.

FIG. 17.—THE FALLS OF NIAGARA.

Toronto, the principal city of Ontario, situated upon Lake Ontario, has a population numbering about 200,000. It is a university town, and an important centre of trade and manufacture.

Kingston also has a large university, and a military college. Many of the young men educated at this college have become officers in the British Army. **London, Hamilton, Guelph,** and **Belleville** are other considerable towns.

"Lumbering."

The whole of Eastern Canada was originally a vast forest. For more than a hundred years the cutting of timber, or "lumber," as it is called in Canada, from these forests, for shipment to Britain and other places, has been one of the principal occupations of the people in large sections of the country, and it is still a very important industry, the export of wood in various forms being greater than that of any other single product of Canada.

Most of this timber is shipped from ports on the River and Gulf of St. Lawrence, and on the Bay of Fundy. The larger portion comes to Liverpool, which is the centre of the Canadian timber trade in England, but some is sent to other British ports. Every summer hundreds of ships and thousands of sailors are employed in carrying this timber from Canadian forests across the Atlantic. In Great Britain it is used for house and ship building, in mines, for manufacturing furniture and machinery, and in many other ways.

The work of getting the timber out of the forests is called "lumbering," and furnishes one of the most picturesque and characteristic aspects of life in Eastern Canada.

The climate of the country is curiously adapted to the necessities of this great industry. At the end of November, or early in December, the severe frosts begin to be felt. These, which in some countries are looked upon as a hardship, here come as the greatest blessing. The ground begins to freeze, and the rivers are covered with ice. The whole surface of the soil, even in the swamps and bogs, becomes as firm as a pavement. Soon the whole country is covered with snow—slightly at first, but gradually the depth becomes greater, with successive snowfalls, as the winter advances.

This is the lumberman's opportunity.

Everywhere through the forest he may drive his teams of horses or oxen, and where he goes the snow quickly becomes compact, making an easy highway over places which in summer are impassable.

During the autumn tracts of forest have been carefully selected for the winter's operations, and out of rough-hewn timber large "camps" or "shanties" have been built, often large enough to accommodate fifty or a hundred men.

As winter puts a stop to work on farms and in the saw-mills, great bodies of labourers find their way to these distant winter homes.

Then the forest, which has been left to utter loneliness through the long drowsy days of summer, becomes for

months a scene of strenuous activity.   On all sides the
axe of the Chopper is heard, as he cuts down tall trees,
which fall with echoing crash, trims off the branches, and
divides the trunks into proper lengths.

Then the large pieces of timber are put on sleds and
hauled to the nearest stream, seldom more than two or
three miles away, on the banks of which they are piled up
in what are called " brows."   A brow often contains
many thousand pieces of timber.

But the timber is still sometimes hundreds of miles
from the mills where it is to be sawn or the ports from
which it is to be shipped.   How does it get there?

Frost and snow prepared the highway over which it
was drawn from its place in the forest to the river bank.
Another change in the seasons prepares a more splendid
highway to serve the lumberman's next purpose.   Spring
draws near—the sun grows more powerful—the snows
melt and fill every brook and river-bed to the brim with a
rushing flood of water.   The lumbermen cut away the
stays and supports of the brows of logs, and the whole
mass tumbles into the stream and is swept down by the
current.   Gangs of " stream-drivers," as the workmen
are now called, follow along the banks to push off the
logs which get caught in the rocks or entangled in the
bushes which border the streams.   Far down the river,
where the current has grown broad and deep, " booms"
are arranged to catch the floating timber.   It is a common
sight to see on the great rivers booms containing many
hundred thousands of logs, and covering many acres of
the water.   Here the logs are sorted, some distinguishing

mark having been put upon each by its owner before it left the forest. They are now formed into large rafts and floated down to the ports or to the saw-mills, where they are cut into boards or "deals" before shipment.

FIG. 18.—STREAM-DRIVING.

Timber not thus sawn is roughly hewn before it leaves the forest, and shipped as "square timber."

Cutting up the Timber.

Most of the logs, however, are prepared for export-ation in the saw-mills. All through the summer months a Canadian saw-mill presents a scene of wonderful activity.

Sometimes the machinery is driven by steam. More often the mill is built beside a water-fall, where the force of the running stream furnishes the necessary power.

One by one the huge logs fresh from the forest are drawn up in rapid succession from the water, and pass into one end of the mill to reappear in a few minutes at the other end ready for the English market. First a carefully arranged set of saws cuts the log into planks or boards of the required thickness ; each of these then goes into the hands of the trimmers, one set of whom with circular saws cuts off the rough edges, and passes it on to others who measure it to proper lengths, cut off the ends, and mark upon each piece its dimensions, after which it is carried at once to the "lumber yard," where it is placed in immense piles awaiting shipment. The better portions of the refuse wood are cut into laths and palings—the remainder is used for fuel. Thus a few minutes is sufficient to change a large, rough pine-tree into shapely planks, ready for the tools of the carpenter.

Lumbermen and backwoodsmen acquire great skill in the use of the axe, and no accomplishment is more useful to anyone living in the newer parts of Eastern Canada. A settler who has this skill can not only clear up the forest, prepare timber for market, and supply himself with fuel with his axe, but almost without the help of other implements he can build his log house and barns, put up fences, construct a bridge over a brook, make a raft or boat to cross larger streams, and do many other equally useful and necessary things.

Maple Sugar.

Another industry peculiar to Eastern Canada and its forests deserves mention. Most of the sugar which people use in this country comes from the sugar-cane, which grows only in hot climates; or from the beet-root, which is much cultivated for this purpose in countries like France and Germany. Now in Canada much sugar is obtained from an entirely different source. The maple is one of the most common of Canadian trees. Its foliage, after being touched by the first autumn frosts, assumes the most brilliant tints of crimson, yellow, and purple, giving a wonderful richness of colouring to Canadian scenery. It is probably for this reason that the maple leaf has been adopted as one of the national emblems of Canada, just as the rose, thistle, and shamrock are taken as the emblems of England, Scotland, and Ireland respectively. But the maple is useful as well as beautiful. In the spring, when the increasing heat of the sun begins to conquer the winter frosts, a sap with a sweet flavour commences to flow in the trunk of the maple tree. Then the farmer or backwoodsman makes a slight incision in the wood, and by inserting a small tube collects the flowing sap in pails or troughs. A single tree will yield from six to twelve quarts on a favourable day, a good flow of sap depending on a warm sunny day following upon a frosty night. The liquid is boiled in large kettles or pans till, by evaporation, it is reduced to the consistency of syrup. If the process is continued the syrup finally

crystallises, when it is moulded into cakes of sugar.
Both syrup and sugar have a peculiarly delicate flavour,
and command in the market much higher prices than the
products of the sugar-cane.

The sugar-making season usually extends through
the month of March, and the annual production of the
maple forests for the whole of Canada is said to be about
20,000,000 pounds of sugar and nearly 1,000,000 gallons
of syrup. To the settlers in early days, when imported
sugar was difficult to get, the products of the maple were
a great comfort, and they are still esteemed luxuries.
The maple is so valuable as fuel that there is danger lest
the sugar industry should be gradually destroyed, unless
attention be given to re-planting the maple groves. A
striking picture of backwoods life in Canada is that which
a "sugary" in the depths of the forest presents at night,
with its rude log "camp" used as a dwelling, the great
fires glowing under the steaming kettles of sap lighting
up the white snow around, while over all rests that intense
stillness peculiar to forests in winter, only broken, perhaps,
by the shout of the solitary sugar-maker as he answers the
whoop of the equally solitary owl. But the sugar-maker is
not always left alone, for a visit to a sugary is a common
form of Canadian winter picnic.

Manitoba.

As we pass westward from the Province of Ontario, we
leave the eastern woodland region, and come out upon the
prairie country of Canada. The first portion of this is
Manitoba, a new province formed in 1870 by the

F

Dominion Parliament out of the wide territories of the North-West. Manitoba has an area of over 60,000 square miles, and is therefore rather larger than England and Wales.

The soil of Manitoba, as of much of the prairie land of Canada, is among the richest in the world; so deep and rich, indeed, that it produces crop after crop for many years without the addition of manure. It is peculiarly adapted for the growth of wheat, which is the most important product of the province. The rapid advance of Manitoba in population and production is shown by the fact that while in 1882 no wheat had been exported, in 1892, ten years later, it produced more than 53,000,000 bushels. Part of this is used in Canada itself, but much is sent down the great lakes and across the Atlantic to England. The soil has been found to be equally well suited for producing other cereal crops and vegetables, as well as for dairy-farming.

Manitoba is covered with a network of rivers and lakes. The largest sheet of water is **Lake Winnipeg,** 278 miles long, and in some places 57 miles broad. The largest rivers are the **Assiniboine** and **Red River,** both navigable streams.

The province is rapidly becoming covered with a network of railways as well, more than 1,200 miles having been constructed within a few years. The chief town, **Winnipeg,** which thirty years ago had scarcely 200 inhabitants, has now more than 60,000. This shows us how an important city may grow up rapidly because it is the centre of a rich farming district.

The North-West Territories.

The prairie country and wheat belt of Canada stretches westward from Manitoba towards the Rocky Mountains. In this vast region four large districts have already been laid off. Their names and area are as follows :—

Assiniboia .	. .	95,000 square miles
Saskatchewan .	. .	100,000 ,, ,,
Alberta . .	. .	111,000 ,, ,,
Athabasca . .	. .	122,000 ,, ,,

In these territories are many millions of acres of fertile lands awaiting cultivation. Great navigable rivers, such as the **Qu'Appelle, Saskatchewan,** and **Peace River,** flow through them, and lakes everywhere abound. This prairie country is believed to comprise the largest unoccupied area of **wheat land** in the world.

Alberta is particularly suited for stock raising, and large districts are leased from Government for grazing purposes, or "ranching" as it is called. Vast herds of cattle feed over the plains which once supported millions of wild buffalo. The latter have entirely disappeared with the settlement of the country.

Alberta has **coal deposits** which are known to cover some thousands of square miles, and mines already opened supply the country east and west with fuel for railway and domestic purposes.

Athabasca forms a part of the great Mackenzie basin. Much of the country immediately north of the prairie belt is as yet unsettled and little known, but recent explorations show that it includes large territories of value for agricultural purposes, as well as for their timber, while

other parts are rich in minerals of many kinds. **Petroleum**·
deposits of great extent have also been found.

Free Lands.

Unoccupied land is so abundant in Canada that the
Governments of the different provinces and that of the
Dominion either give to the emigrants who come to settle
in the country enough to make a farm or sell it to them
at a very low price.

Emigrants who wish to settle on these unoccupied
lands can choose between two different ways of beginning
life as farmers in Canada. They may go into the parts of
the country which are covered with forest, which has to be
cleared away before crops can be grown. Here there is
much severe labour in preparing the ground for cultivation,
but there is also the great advantage of having abundance of
fuel close at hand, timber for constructing houses, barns,
and fences, and employment during the winter months
when the tillage of the ground is stopped by frost. Or
they may prefer to go upon the western prairies, where the
land is often without trees, and ready at once for the
plough. Here fuel and timber must be brought from
a considerable distance, but the raising of crops can at
once be easily begun. In either case industrious men
can soon make for themselves comfortable homes, and find
themselves the possessors of good farms.

British Columbia.

The large Province of **British Columbia**, which lies
along the Pacific Coast of the Dominion, is about three

times the size of Great Britain and Ireland. Its great
extent may be illustrated in another way by pointing out
that it is equal in area to France, Italy, Belgium, and
Holland all put together. In many ways British Columbia
differs from the other provinces of the Dominion. It has
been described as a sea of mountains. The great range of
the Rockies stretches along its eastern border. From
this westward to the Pacific there is nothing like a plain
or prairie, but range after range of lofty mountains succeed
each other, with here and there fertile valleys lying
between. The scenery of the Pacific Coast is remarkable;
Lord Dufferin thus described it after a visit in 1876:—

A Picture of the Pacific Coast.

"Such a spectacle as its coast-line presents is
not to be paralleled by any country in the world. Day
after day for a whole week, in a vessel of nearly
2,000 tons, we threaded an interminable labyrinth of
watery lanes and reaches that wound endlessly in and out
of a network of islands, promontories, and peninsulas for
thousands of miles, unruffled by the slightest swell from
the adjoining ocean, and presenting at every turn an ever-
shifting combination of rock, verdure, forest, glacier, and
snow-capped mountain of unrivalled grandeur and beauty.
When it is remembered that this wonderful system of
navigation, equally well adapted to the largest line-of-
battle ship and the frailest canoe, fringes the entire seaboard of the province, and communicates at points, sometimes more than a hundred miles from the coast, with
a multitude of valleys stretching eastward into the

interior. while, at the same time, it is furnished with innumerable harbours on either hand, one is lost in admiration at the facilities for intercommunication which are thus provided for the inhabitants of this wonderful region."

The Products of British Columbia.

The coast waters which are thus described have important and valuable **fisheries**. Equally remarkable are those of the rivers. The picture on the opposite page will help us to understand why so many of the cases of tinned salmon which we see in grocers' windows are marked as coming from British Columbia.

The forest trees grow to an extraordinary size. The Douglas fir, especially, is often found 300 feet in height, and with a diameter of eight or nine feet. Large quantities of **timber** are shipped to Australia, Asia, South America, and Africa, as well as to England.

In the heart of the mountains and up the valleys of the great rivers minerals of many kinds are found. Gold to the amount of £10,000,000 was a few years ago taken from the river-beds in a short time. Important discoveries of both gold and silver have lately been made in the Kootenay District, near the southern boundary, in the Cariboo District farther north, and on the Klondyke in the Yukon district, so that British Columbia now promises to become one of the richest mining countries in the world.

The coal mines of **Vancouver Island** and of the Rocky Mountains are important, and will be spoken of in another chapter, when we speak of the coal supplies of the Empire.

Owing to warm currents from the Pacific Ocean, the

climate of the western parts of British Columbia is milder
than that of other parts of Canada, and the average tem-

FIG. 19.—BRITISH COLUMBIAN SALMON RIVER.

perature of places on the coast of the Pacific is ten degrees
higher than in places with the same latitude on the

Atlantic coast. In a mountainous country the variations of temperature are very great, and it is in British Columbia a curious experience to travel by railway in a single day from the snow-covered summits of the Rocky Mountains to the sunny valleys of the coast, where the fields are green and the trees covered with the flowers and tender foliage of spring.

Victoria, the capital of the province, is a city beautifully situated on Vancouver Island.

The town of **Vancouver**, on the mainland, has risen rapidly into importance within the last few years. We shall have more to say about it when we come to speak of our voyage across the Pacific. **Esquimalt**, a fine harbour three miles from Victoria, has a large graving-dock for the repair of ships, and is the station for our war-ships in the North Pacific. It is now strongly fortified.

The Great Fur Land.

If we look again at the map of Canada we see that parts of it stretch far up into the frozen regions of the North. Here the summers are too short and the climate too cold for farming. But it must not for this reason be supposed that it is a useless country or one where people cannot find occupation.

Around **Hudson Bay** and the thousands of lakes, great and small, which are scattered over this vast region, and along the rivers which flow into the Arctic Ocean and Hudson Bay, is the great fur country of Canada. Nature has here provided animals with warm coats of the finest fur with which to endure the intense cold of winter, and it is from these regions that very many of those beautiful

furs come which ladies wear, and which we see exposed
for sale in the shop-windows of our large towns.

The management of this fur trade has long been chiefly
in the hands of a company of English merchants called the
Hudson Bay Company. All over the country, from the
Hudson Bay to the Arctic Ocean on the North and the
Pacific on the West, this company has posts or forts where
agents are stationed to buy the furs from the white or
Indian trappers by whom the animals are caught. A
solitary and adventurous life the trapper leads, often
spending months of the long winter alone in the remotest
parts of the forest. When the trapping season is over he
brings the furs he has obtained to the Company's nearest
post, to be exchanged for clothing, blankets, guns,
powder, and other necessaries of his simple existence. In
the summer, when the rivers and lakes are free from ice,
the furs are packed in bales and sent in canoes, managed
by a class of hardy and skilful boatmen, called *voyageurs*,
many hundreds of miles to the ports from which they are
shipped to England. In London they are sold by auction,
and soon they are made up into garments of various kinds
to make comfortable those who can afford to buy them.

NOTE.—Northern Canada has been called "the last great fur reserve
of the world." The importance of the fur trade may be judged from the
fact that between four and five millions of skins are every year offered for
sale in the London market, chiefly by the Hudson Bay Company. Among
them are included those of the otter, beaver, bear, grey and silver fox, the
marten, mink, ermine, and sable, some of which are considered among the
most rich and valuable furs in the world. Nor are furs all which this
cold Northern region produces. The lakes and rivers team with fish of
many kinds, while the neighbouring seas contain whales, walruses, and
seals, valuable for their oils or skins.

So we find that even the coldest and most distant parts of Canada furnish something for the comfort of people in this country.

Having now completed our short study of Canada, we must visit the smaller colonies along the Atlantic coast of America.

* * *

CHAPTER V.

THE ATLANTIC COAST.

Newfoundland and Labrador.

Newfoundland, the large island lying across the mouth of the Gulf of St. Lawrence, and by which we passed in coming from England to Canada, is the oldest of England's colonies. It was taken possession of for Great Britain by Sir Humphrey Gilbert in 1583, and this date may therefore be looked upon as the starting point of the wonderful growth of the Empire and spread of our British people over the world.

The " French Shore."

Settlements were not made, however, for many years after it was annexed, and all through the seventeenth century we had to contend with the French for its possession. Our right to the island was finally acknowledged by the Treaty of Utrecht in 1713. Unfortunately the French were allowed to retain certain rights along what is called the " **French Shore**," extending from Cape St. John on the east coast around the north of the island to Cape Ray in the south-west. This circumstance has hindered the settlement of this portion of the country, and given rise to serious disputes; but English and French statesmen in 1904 concluded a treaty which settled these differences.

Newfoundland is larger than Ireland, having an area of more than 42,000 square miles.

The population, including that of the neighbouring dependency of **Labrador,** numbers about 220,000, and is settled chiefly in the south-eastern part of the island. The inland parts are as yet without inhabitants.

The capital town, **St. John,** has about 30,000 inhabitants. It depends for its prosperity almost entirely upon the fisheries.

The Newfoundland Fisheries.

For more than three centuries Newfoundland has been famed for its **cod-fisheries,** which are the most productive in the world. The cod is found along the whole coast, but is caught in the greatest numbers on what are known as the "Banks," a large area of the neighbouring ocean where the sea is unusually shallow, varying from 50 to 350 feet in depth.

To these banks in the summer hundreds of fishing vessels come from all parts, and immense numbers of fish are caught. When salted and dried, the cod are exported, chiefly to the Mediterranean, the West Indies, and South America. The cod-liver oil, obtained, as its name tells us, from the liver of the cod, is, as we know, much used as a medicine, and also forms an important article of commerce.

Seal-fishing is also a considerable industry. In the early spring the sealing vessels push northward among the floes of ice which then cover the sea, and on which the seals rear their young. Here they are sometimes killed in such numbers that a single steam sailing vessel has brought home £30,000 worth of blubber and seal-skins. At other times the catch is small.

The coast waters abound with other kinds of fish, the most important of which are **herring** and **salmon**. The **lobster** fishery along the French Shore is important enough to have formed one of the chief points of dispute with France.

The people of Newfoundland, then, rely chiefly for their subsistence upon " the harvest of the sea."

The island has other resources, which will be developed by the railway lately completed from St. John through the heart of the country to the west coast. Parts of the island are known to be rich in minerals of different kinds : iron-ore is particularly abundant, and there has long been a considerable export of copper-ore.

It is hoped that Newfoundland will one day become a province of the Dominion of Canada.

Labrador.

The eastern portion of Labrador is governed as a de-pendency of Newfoundland. Its wild uncultivated coast has a scattered population consisting of a few thousands of Esquimaux, Indians, and whites, who are occupied almost entirely in fishing and hunting.

Bermuda.

We now pass further south into a warmer climate.

Out in the Atlantic, 600 miles from the coast of North

America, and about half-way between Eastern Canada and the West Indies, lies the group of islands known as **Bermuda**, or **The Bermudas**. These islands have formed a part of the Empire since 1609, when they were first occupied by some shipwrecked English sailors. They have now become of great value to us as a naval station.

During the cold of the Canadian winter and the extreme heat of the West Indian summer our ships of war visit Bermuda for the sake of the temperate and healthful climate. A great deal of money has been spent in protecting the channel which leads into the main harbour by fortifications and batteries of heavy guns, and we usually keep here about 1,500 soldiers. An enemy would now find it a very difficult task to capture Bermuda.

For the repair of large ships an immense floating dock was constructed some years ago in this country and taken to Bermuda. It is 381 feet long, 84 feet broad, and 53 feet deep—large enough to hold one of the large ironclads of the Royal Navy.

The climate of Bermuda is so mild and agreeable that the islands have become a winter resort for invalids from the American continent. As there are no winter frosts, agriculture can be carried on continually, and three crops of potatoes can be raised during the year. The inhabitants, who number about 17,500, are chiefly engaged in raising vegetables for export to the United States and Canada. The whole area of the 360 islands which make up the group is only about 12,000 acres, and not more than a third of the land is fit for cultivation; but from this limited space the markets of the neighbouring continent are largely supplied with vegetables some weeks before those of home production are fit for use.

The West Indies.

America, or the New World as it was then called, was discovered by Christopher Columbus about 400 years ago (1492).

When that great navigator sailed away from Europe across the Atlantic, he expected to come to India. He supposed that the islands to which he first came were off the Indian coast, and hence they got the name of the West Indies.

Columbus was equipped for his voyage by the King and Queen of Spain, and so Spain at first claimed all the West Indian Islands by right of this discovery. But the other nations of Europe soon became very anxious to get a footing there. Spain had drawn much wealth from her new possessions in America, and the islands were the first places from which the productions of the Tropics were brought into common use in Europe. Sugar and molasses, rum and tobacco, fruits and spices, valuable woods and dyes could all be procured in the West Indies, and the leading European nations were eager to have a share in the profitable trade in these articles. So for nearly three centuries a constant struggle went on for the possession of the islands, and many of them were captured and retaken several times by the contending nations.

In these struggles our own British people took a large part. At first merchants and private adventurers went to carry on trade and make settlements on some of the smaller islands. Thus several important colonies were formed, which we hold by right of settlement.

Later, when England at different times was at war in Europe with Spain, France, or Holland, she usually conquered and took possession of islands in the West Indies belonging to these Powers. The result has been that although Spain, France, Holland, Sweden, and Denmark all share with us in the possession of the West Indian Islands, we hold by far the larger number of them. The area of the British islands, however, is surpassed by that of the two great islands, Cuba and Porto Rico.

Climate of the West Indies.

When we look at a map or globe we see that the West India Islands are nearly all situated within the **Tropics**— that is, between the Tropic of Cancer and the Tropic of Capricorn, the two circles which form the northern and southern limits of the Torrid Zone. We know that the climate of tropical countries is usually very hot. In some British possessions, of which we shall have to speak further on, the heat is so great that they are unfit for Europeans to settle in.

White people go there for a time to trade or to carry on the Government, but do not form permanent homes. This is not the case with the West Indies. The tropical heat is there so moderated by sea-breezes and other influences that the islands have been regularly colonised by Europeans, whose descendants have remained there for many generations. But while the heat does not prevent white people from settling in the West Indies, it does make it very difficult for them to perform severe manual labour.

For this labour they have to depend upon the coloured races, who are by nature fitted to endure great heat.

Slavery.

When the Spaniards first discovered the West Indies they found them inhabited by Indian races, most of whom were gentle and peaceable, but not capable of enduring severe labour. Vast numbers of these earlier inhabitants were enslaved by the Spaniards and sent to toil in the mines, where they perished from over-work and other hardships. Others were destroyed in war, and before many years had passed the native population of the islands was almost exterminated.

At a later period, when a great demand had arisen in Europe for sugar, coffee, cotton, and other tropical productions, it became necessary to find a new supply of coloured people to work on the plantations. It was this which led to the introduction of negroes and the spread of negro slavery throughout all the West Indies.

Englishmen, as well as Spaniards, Portuguese, French and Dutch, turned their attention to the trade in slaves.

Hundreds of thousands of negroes were kidnapped, captured in war, or purchased on the coast of Africa, brought across the Atlantic, sold in the slave-markets, and sent to work upon the plantations. Dreadful cruelties were often committed in procuring these slaves in Africa, in carrying them across the ocean, and in their treatment afterwards.

It was a long time, however, before the people of

England were aroused to understand all the sin and shame connected with the slave-trade. But great and good men such as Wilberforce, Fowell Buxton, and others, denounced it in Parliament, and societies were everywhere formed to assist in putting it down.

At last, in 1807, the slave-trade was declared to be unlawful, and in 1834 a Bill was passed in Parliament by which all slaves in countries under British rule were set free, while £20,000,000 was given out of the public funds to repay the slave-owners for what the law had before recognised as their property.

We see, then, that the possession of colonies in the West Indies first led British people into the great wrong of slave-holding, and afterwards rendered it necessary for them to make great sacrifices to set this wrong right.

Slavery was abolished, but work still had to be done if the islands were to be prosperous.

It is easy to understand that the negroes who for so many years had been degraded by slavery, and often with great cruelty compelled by their masters to work, did not know how to make the best use of their new liberty; many were so idle and improvident that for a long time after the abolition of slavery and its cheap forced labour it seemed as if the old industries could not be successfully carried on. In some islands there has now been great improvement, and the negroes have become more industrious. If this has not always been the case, still English people ought to be very patient with the failings of a race which they degraded by slavery for so long a time.

G

Coolie Labour.

In some of the West Indian colonies, where a regular and sufficient supply of negro labourers could not be obtained, **coolies**, or East Indian workmen, have been imported in great numbers. The coolies are found to be very steady and industrious, and they work for low wages. Before leaving India they make an agreement to work for a certain number of years in the colony to which they go, and after the expiration of this term they have a right to be sent back to their own country. Great numbers, however, prefer to remain, so that in some parts of the West Indies there is a large and increasing population of people of East Indian birth. We shall find that the same thing is true of some other British colonies.

Great precautions are taken that the evils of slavery may not be renewed in connection with coolie labour. In India, the country from which they are brought, the Government is careful to see that the coolies emigrate only at their own desire, that they understand clearly the nature of the bargain they make and the service they have to perform, and that they are well cared for on their long ocean voyage.

The Government of the colony to which they come takes charge of them on their arrival, distributes them among the employers who require their services, and sees that provision is made on every estate for the sick, that the bargain is fairly carried out on both sides, and that when his period of service is expired the coolie is sent back to his native land, if he so desire. All these precautions are necessary, for long experience has shown that white men are too often willing to deal unjustly with the weaker coloured races. We can see, too, how important it is that we should always have just and prudent officers both in India and in the colonies to which coolies are sent, to carry out the wise laws made to protect these labourers.

"Black and White" in the West Indies.

Besides the great numbers of negroes who are descended from former slaves, and the East Indians who are being introduced under the coolie system, there are also scattered through most of the islands many descendants of the early Spanish and French settlers. The population is therefore of a very mixed kind, and the people of British birth probably do not number more than a tenth of the whole. The proportion of white people to black has been decreasing during the last few years.

From what has now been said we can understand how very different things are in tropical colonies like the West Indies from what they are in Canada, Australia, or other parts of the Empire where the people are chiefly of British or European descent.

The Groups of Islands.

The British West Indian Islands are divided for purposes of government into six colonies or sets of colonies. These are—

1. The **Bahamas**.
2. **Jamaica**, with its little dependencies of the **Turk's** and **Caicos** Islands and the **Caymans**.

3. The **Leeward Islands**.

4. **Barbadoes**.

5. The **Windward Islands**.

6. **Trinidad** and **Tobago**.

The map shows that these colonies are not grouped together in any one part of the West Indian archi-

FIG. 26.—THE WEST INDIES, HONDURAS, AND BRITISH GUIANA.

pelago, but are scattered along the whole range of islands from **Florida** to the mouth of the **Orinoco** and in the **Caribbean Sea**. Some of the islands have been built up from the bed of the ocean by the slow labour of the coral insect; others have been thrown up by volcanoes, and, as they are usually covered by luxuriant vegetation, they present a great variety of beautiful scenery. As a rule, the soil is very fertile. The hilly districts are healthy; where the lands are low and wet, as is often the case along the coasts, yellow fever prevails, and is very dangerous for Europeans. Like most tropical islands, the West Indies suffer severely at times from hurricanes. We who live in a temperate climate like that of the British Islands can form little idea of the terrible force of the wind in a West Indian hurricane, when it not only destroys the crops, but sweeps away houses, and uproots or breaks down whole forests, leaving behind it a scene of utter ruin. Fortunately some islands are fairly free from hurricanes, and in others they only occur at intervals of several years. Once past, the people set themselves to work to repair the harm that has been done.

What we get from the West Indies.

The productions of the islands are so numerous that it would be difficult to mention them all. Among the principal ones are sugar, coffee, cocoa, tobacco, cotton, mahogany, logwood, ginger, vanilla, allspice, cloves, cassia, indigo, aloes, sarsaparilla, maize, rice, arrow-root, tapioca, and tropical fruits of many kinds, particularly bananas and pine-apples. When you think how many of these things cannot be produced in Britain, and yet how constantly we use them, you can understand how much we depend on countries like the West Indies for the comforts of our daily life.

We may now give a short account of each of the groups into which our West Indian colonies are divided.

The Bahamas.

This group consists of about twenty inhabited islands and numberless cays and rocks, with an area in all of 5,794 square miles.

The **Bahamas** extend from Florida over about 600 miles of sea along the northern coast of Cuba. The climate is so good that some of the islands have become a favourite winter residence for invalids. The white people number only about one in four in the whole population. **Oranges, bananas,** and **pine apples** are raised in large quantities, and sponges are procured from the sea. Lately much attention has been paid to cultivating a kind of **aloe** which produces a fibre resembling hemp, and this is fast becoming an important industry in the islands.

The Bahamas were originally settled by English colonists, and they have never passed out of our hands. The little island of San Salvador is supposed to have been the first spot where Columbus landed in the New World.

Jamaica.

Jamaica is the largest of the British West Indian islands. It is 144 miles long, 49 miles broad at its widest point, and it has an area of 4,193 square miles. The **Blue Mountains** extend through the interior, and at one point rise to the height of 7,360 feet. This mountainous character of the inland districts is a great advantage to the island, since it gives a variety of climate and production, and enables the inhabitants of the low and hot districts nearer the coast to find close at hand a complete change of scene and air. In the higher mountainous districts the air is so cold that fires are usually found necessary for comfort. The result of this varied climate is that Jamaica is, in parts, better suited for European settlement than most of the other West Indian Islands. There are, however, at the present time less than 15,000 whites in a population of about 770,000.

Jamaica was originally settled by the Spaniards, under whose rule the large Carib population was almost entirely destroyed, and negroes were introduced instead. It was captured by England in 1655, when Cromwell, as Protector, was waging war against Spain.

Kingston, the capital of Jamaica, is situated upon an excellent harbour, which forms our principal coaling and naval station in the West Indies. The harbour, which is already strongly fortified, will become of even greater importance than it now is should the completion of the **Panama Canal** make a new route for trade with Australia and the Pacific coasts of America.

Under the government of Jamaica are a few smaller islands. Of these the **Caymans** are a group of coral islands off the southern coast of Cuba, with a small coloured population, chiefly engaged in turtle-fishing and the trade in **timber** and **dye-woods. Turk's Island** and **Caicos,** settled originally from the Bahamas, and more naturally connected with that group, have been annexed since 1873 to Jamaica. They are chiefly noted for their large production and export of **salt.**

The Leeward Islands.

The **Leeward** group includes **Antigua, Montserrat, Nevis, St. Kitts, Dominica,** the **Virgin Islands,** and a few small dependencies. Each of the larger islands has a local Council for the management of its affairs, with a federal Council and Government for the whole group. The total

area is about 705 square miles. All the islands are mountainous, and some volcanic. St. John's, the largest town
and the seat of the federal Government, is in Antigua.

In Montserrat special attention is paid to the cultivation of the lime; and lime juice, considered the best in the
world, is a chief article of commerce.

Barbadoes.

Barbadoes, which has always been a British colony
since its first settlement in 1625, is one of the most
interesting and prosperous of the West Indian Islands.
It is about the size of the Isle of Wight, and on this small
area has 195,000 people, so that it is one of the most densely
inhabited districts in the world. The island is chiefly
given up to the growth of the sugar-cane, and almost
every acre is carefully cultivated. It has suffered much
at times from hurricanes, but the healthy and equable
climate has been favourable to European settlement, and
it has always had a larger proportion of white inhabitants
than the other islands. Bridgetown, the capital, has a
large trade.

The Windward Islands.*

The Windward Islands include St. Lucia, St. Vincent,
Grenada, and the Grenadines.

St. Lucia has been selected as the second British coaling
station for the West Indies; a large sum of money has been

---

* The terms "Windward" and "Leeward" have been variously
applied in the West Indies at different times. Originally they were
meant to distinguish between the islands (windward) more exposed to the
prevailing north-east trade winds, and those (leeward) less exposed to them.
The division used in this book is more limited, and is that now officially
employed to designate islands grouped together for purposes of government

spent upon the wharves and other works required to make its
chief harbour, **Port Castries,** suitable for this purpose, and
fortifications are also being constructed for the defence
of the port. In **Grenada** much attention is paid to the
cultivation of **cocoa** and spices. Several of the islands are
of volcanic origin, and **St. Vincent** contains an active volcano.

Trinidad.

Trinidad, situated near the coast of South America, is
second only to Jamaica among the British West Indian
Islands in size and importance. It is about 48 miles long
and 35 broad, its area is 1,754 square miles, and its population about 250,000. Settled by the Spaniards, it was
conquered in 1797 by Sir Ralph Abercrombie, and has ever
since remained under British rule. Since the abolition of
slavery large numbers of Indian coolies have been brought
into the country, and they now form a considerable part of
the population. Besides producing sugar, cocoa, coffee,
and the fruits of the Tropics in large quantities, the island
has resources in **timber** and **minerals.** One of its most
remarkable features is a large lake of **asphalt** or **bitumen.**
More than 50,000 tons of this asphalt are sometimes exported in a single year to Europe and America, where it is used
for making sidewalks to the streets and for other purposes.

Tobago, a neighbouring island, with very similar productions, and with a population numbering about 20,000, is for
purposes of government connected with the colony of Trinidad.

Confederation of the West India Islands.

In speaking of Canada, it was pointed out that
more than twenty years ago all the provinces, formerly

separate colonies, united themselves into one Dominion, with a single Parliament to manage their more important affairs. Many believe that a similar union would be of great advantage to the West Indian Islands. In earlier times, when communication between them was slow and difficult, a common government would have been impossible. Now, however, all the principal islands are connected by the telegraph, as well as by lines of steamships, and the similarity of their productions gives them many common commercial interests which it is thought could be best managed by a central Government acting for all the colonies.

British Honduras.

Besides our island possessions in the West Indies, we have two important colonies on the neighbouring mainland.

British Honduras is westward of Jamaica, on the coast of Central America. It has an area of 7,562 square miles, and a population numbering about 37,100.

For more than 200 years this coast has been famous for its **mahogany** and **logwood**, the one so much used in making furniture, the other as a dye, and it was for the sake of the trade in these and other woods that we occupied and have retained Honduras.

For many years the early settlers carried on a stubborn contest with the Spaniards for the possession of the country and the right of cutting timber in the forests. In 1798 a strong Spanish force was sent to drive the English out of the country, but this force was defeated, and since that time it has remained a British colony, and its limits have been gradually extended.

The fact that in 1901 more than 19,600 tons of log-wood and 6,485,952 cubic feet of mahogany were exported, chiefly to the United Kingdom, shows how valuable the trade in wood still is. While mahogany and logwood are likely to continue to be the staple productions of Honduras, the soil is said to be one of the most fertile in the world, and fitted to produce in perfection all the fruits of the Tropics. There is already a small export of **sugar, coffee, bananas,** and **cocoanuts,** but the agricultural development of the country has only lately begun.

British Guiana.

Forming a part of our West Indian system of colonies, but situated upon the mainland of South America, and close to the Equator, is **British Guiana,** for the possession of which Britain had many contests with France and Holland. These countries still possess large adjoining districts, known as Dutch and French Guiana. The portion under British rule is nearly as large as the United Kingdom, and was finally secured to us by the Treaty of Paris in 1814.

Guiana is the only territory which we possess on the South American continent. It is a rich colony, and its wealth has come almost entirely from one great industry, the production of **sugar.** Great sugar estates stretch for miles along the sea-coast and the banks of the great rivers. These estates are chiefly owned by people in London, the work upon them is done by Indian coolies and other coloured labourers, and few landowners are settled in the country. This is probably due to the climate, which, on the coast, is more trying to Europeans than that of the islands, where the heat is tempered by the sea-breezes from all sides.

A recent writer says of Guiana :—

"The flat alluvial country along the coast is so well adapted to the growth of the sugar-cane that sugar has become the one absorbing industry of the colony. More capital and greater enterprise have been brought to bear upon sugar-growing in British Guiana than in any other part of the British Empire. The Demerara sugars have in consequence a world-wide name : they were the first West Indian sugar to be brought into the English market ready for consumption without further refining, and they have been taken as a standard by sugar growers and refiners elsewhere. In 1888 the colony exported 110,000 tons of sugar, and, though this was a short crop, it was not much less than half of the total sugar export of the British West Indies."

Gold-mines have also been found in the inland parts, and in 1901 more than £371,100 worth was exported, so that gold-mining has become an important industry in the colony.

El Dorado.

The finding of gold here recalls the famous story of El Dorado, the City of Gold, which was once connected in men's minds with Guiana.

More than 300 years ago a Spanish soldier, one of an exploring expedition up the Orinoco, was set adrift by his companions, and when, after many months, he found his way back to his own countrymen, he reported that he had

been taken by Indians to a great inland lake with golden
sands, on which stood a vast city roofed with gold.
Excited by the discoveries of gold which they had actually
made in Peru, many of the Spaniards were ready to believe
this fable, and eager adventurers kept exploring South
America all through the sixteenth century in search of
the City of Gold. It is needless to say that they never
found what they sought. But we read in history how
even a great Englishman, Sir Walter Raleigh, who had
done much in founding colonies for Britain, had his
imagination so filled with these stories of undiscovered
wealth that he himself conducted two expeditions, and
sent out others, to explore the rivers and coast of Guiana
for the gold-mines supposed to be there.

The Falkland Islands.

Sailing far away to the south we come to the
Falkland Islands, which lie about 480 miles north-east
of Cape Horn, and are the most southern inhabited British
dependency. The total area of the islands is about 6,500
square miles, and the population numbers about 2,040.
It was finally established as a British colony about fifty or
sixty years ago, after several unsuccessful attempts by the
French and Spaniards to form settlements. The station is
useful at times to ships trading around Cape Horn, or
engaged in the whale fisheries, and in time of war its
possession might become of considerable importance from a
naval point of view.

At present the chief employment of the people is sheep
raising, and the exports consist almost entirely of wool,

live sheep, frozen mutton, hides, and tallow. The pasturage is excellent, but the cloudy skies and frequent rains make it impossible for grain to ripen.

South Georgia, about 800 miles to the south-east of the Falklands, was taken possession of by Captain Cook in 1775. It was once the resort of sealing vessels, but is now uninhabited. This group of islands is supposed to have an area of 1,000 square miles, and though it is sometimes spoken of as a dependency of the Falklands, it cannot be considered as having any value to the Empire.

•••

CHAPTER VI.

THE PACIFIC COAST.

WE have now completed our short survey of those parts of the Empire which are on or near the American continent, and we return to the Pacific coast of Canada to resume our journey around the world. Our point of departure is **Vancouver** in British Columbia.

Vancouver.

We must say something more about this town of Vancouver, for two reasons: first, because we are making it a fresh starting-place in our tour around the Empire, and second, because its history makes us understand what great changes are rapidly taking place in the newer and more distant parts of the Empire.

In 1886 the ground where Vancouver now stands was covered with a dense forest, composed chiefly of trees of extraordinary size. A single house was the only sign of human habitation. Now, after a few years, it has a population of more than 25,000 people, and where the forest stood are to be seen many miles of fine streets, with churches, hotels, shops, and comfortable homes. Steamships are unloading their cargoes at the wharves, and trains are arriving at the busy railway station or leaving it with passengers and merchandise.

The Canadian Pacific Railway.

What has caused this sudden and wonderful change? The reason is that on account of the excellent harbour close at hand Vancouver was selected as the terminus of the great railway which crosses Canada, and also as the starting-place for the steamship lines which carry on trade across the Pacific. People soon saw that it was to be an important centre of commerce, and so they flocked thither in great numbers.

Let us go down beside the harbour in Vancouver and watch the large steamship which is discharging its cargo into a train of cars waiting upon the wharf. We find that the vessel has just arrived from Yokohama in Japan, and that she is chiefly laden with tea. The tea will be at once sent across the continent to Eastern Canada or to the United States. When the steamship has been unloaded she will prepare for her return voyage to Japan and China. Notice that besides freight and passengers she will carry the mails which have just arrived from England. These mails will reach Japan more speedily than they could by any other way.

The Shortest Route to the Far East.

We have seen before that the shortest route across the Atlantic is that from **Great Britain** to **Halifax** or **Quebec**; that the shortest railway line across the continent of America is that from **Quebec** to **Vancouver**; and now we can add that the shortest steamship route across the Pacific is that from **Vancouver** to **Yokohama**. From London to Yokohama the distance, by crossing Canada, is about 10,060 miles, or nearly 1,000 miles less than by way of New York and San Francisco, and it is far shorter than over the eastern route by way of the Suez Canal and Singapore. So England's new way across Canada to the East is the shortest of all. Useful as it now is for carrying mails, passengers, and commerce, it might become even more important should the Suez Canal be closed in time of war.

Something more should be said about the steamship which is leaving Vancouver for Yokohama, for she belongs to a class of vessels in which British people have a special interest. In the first place, as she is intended to carry the mails, she is built to steam rapidly. For a long voyage and at ordinary times she is planned to go at the rate of 16½ knots an hour, and, if necessary, she can go much faster. At her usual rate of speed she carries the mails across the Pacific to Yokohama in ten or eleven days.

Observe next that the captain and some of the officers wear the letters R.N.R. upon their uniforms. This means that they belong to the **Royal Naval Reserve**, and may in time of war be called upon to serve in the Royal Navy, for the duties of which they have been trained and examined.

Again, the ship has been so built that in a very short time she can have guns placed in position upon her, and so be changed into an armed cruiser or ship of war. Guns for this purpose are kept in store at Vancouver, and also

FIG. 21.—GUN PRACTICE UPON A MERCANTILE CRUISER.

at Hong Kong, the English port of the China seas. Should war unfortunately break out between ourselves and any other Power this change would at once be made, when the ship would be ready to defend herself, inflict damage on the enemy, or carry troops or war stores to any point where they were required.

Our Government every year pays a large sum of money to the owners of fast steamships of this class, on the

II

Atlantic and Indian Oceans as well as the Pacific, partly for carrying the mails, and partly for holding their ships thus in readiness to become armed cruisers.

It is believed that these ships would add greatly to the safety of our commerce in any sudden outbreak of war.

Across the Pacific.

The voyage from Canada to Australasia is a long one, more than 6,500 miles, for we have to cross the Pacific, the largest of the oceans. On a good steamship, however, the voyage can be made in less than three weeks. In these three weeks we find that we have passed from one season of the year to another. All places in the Northern Hemisphere—that is, the half of the world between the North Pole and the Equator—have seasons opposite to those of corresponding places in the Southern Hemisphere. When there is winter north of the Equator there is summer to the south of it, and when the northern summer begins then winter sets in at the south.

So, again, if you leave Canada in the early spring, you find, when you arrive three weeks later in New Zealand or Australia, that it is the beginning of the southern autumn. In British Columbia the leaves are beginning to burst forth; in New Zealand the fruits of autumn are being gathered. One result of this change of season we ought to note. As we visit various colonies we find that in their different climates almost every variety of food is produced. But this is not all. The difference of season in the Northern and Southern Hemispheres brings it about that grains and fruits are coming to perfection in different parts of the Empire in different months of the year. This is another kind of variety within the Empire which leads to trade between ourselves and our own people abroad to the advantage of both.

A Lost Day.

We must not forget to note a curious fact connected with voyaging across the Pacific. At a certain longitude (180°) as you travel westward a day of the week and of the month is dropped from the reckoning of time. Going to bed, for instance, on Wednesday night, you awake next day to find it is Friday morning. When you arrive in New Zealand or Australia you find that this new arrangement of the days corresponds with what is being used there. The old navigators who first went around the world were much puzzled to find when they returned to Europe that they had lost a day in their reckoning.

NOTE.- When the voyage across the Pacific is eastward, instead of dropping a day from the calendar, one is added to it. Mr. Froude, in " Oceana," says :—" Time and its tenses are strange things, and at their strangest when one is travelling round the globe. The question is not only what season is it, but what day is it, and what o'clock is it? The Captain *makes* it twelve o'clock when he tells us that it is noon; and it seemed as if a supply of time was among the ship's stores, for when we reached 180° East longitude, he presented us with an extra day, and we had two Thursdays—two eighths of April—in one week. As our course was eastward, we met the sun each morning before it would rise at the point where we had been on the morning before; and the day was, therefore, shorter than the complete period of the globe's revolution. Each degree of longitude represented a loss of four minutes, and the total loss in a complete circuit would be an entire day of twenty-four hours. We had gone through half of it, and the captain owed us twelve hours. He paid us these, and advanced us twelve more, which we should have spent or paid back to him by the time that we reached Liverpool."

Perhaps this will seem clearer if put in another way.

An Empire upon which the Sun never sets.

We sometimes hear it said that the sun never sets upon our British Empire. Here is a diagram which

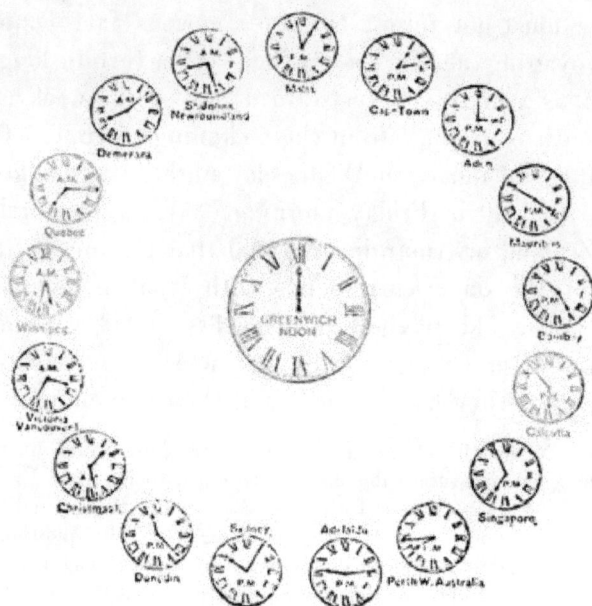

FIG. 22.—THE TIME OF DAY THROUGHOUT THE EMPIRE.

enables us to understand this better by pointing out the hour of the day in various parts of the colonies when it is noon at Greenwich near London.

A British Pacific Cable.

Fanning Island is the first British possession which we come to in crossing the Pacific. It is one of several groups of small islands, lying in the Pacific, on the route between Canada and Australasia, which have been annexed to the Empire, during the last few years, to secure them for use as **telegraph stations.** A cable across the Pacific was completed on October 31st, 1902, and Canada and Australia have now telegraphic connection with each other. England by this means is in cable communication with her most distant colonies by a western, as well as an eastern route, the new line having the advantage of passing exclusively over British soil. Starting from Vancouver, Fanning Island, the Fiji Islands, and Norfolk Island are successively reached. Then the cable divides, one branch going to Brisbane, the other to New Zealand.

From Vancouver a line of steamships carries passengers and freight from Canada to New Zealand and Australia. The growing commerce of these great colonies makes this route one of much importance. By this line, too, letters can now be sent from the United Kingdom across the Atlantic, Canada, and the Pacific to New Zealand and some parts of Australia even more quickly than they are forwarded by way of the Suez Canal.

The Fiji Islands.

Our largest and most interesting possession in Polynesia is the **Fiji** group of islands, situated between 15° and 20° south of the **Equator.**

The area of all the Islands, of which there are more than 200, is 7,740 square miles, and the inhabitants number more than 117,000, of whom nearly 2,500 are

Europeans. Fiji was voluntarily ceded to the Queen in
1874 by the native chiefs and people, who had for some
time desired to place themselves under British rule. It
was then organised as a Crown colony; but care has been
taken to respect the customs of the people, annual

FIG. 23.—A SCENE IN FIJI.
(From a Photograph by Henry King of Sydney.)

meetings of the chiefs and representatives of the different
districts are held, and as far as possible the management
of local affairs is left in their own hands. In productions
and climate the Fiji Islands much resemble the West
Indies. **Sugar** is now the most important export,
but **fruit** and **cocoa-nuts** are also largely raised,
and find a market in Britain, New Zealand, and

Australia. **Tea. coffee, cotton,** and **maize** are also produced.

Though near the Equator, Fiji has a climate which is not specially unfavourable to Europeans, the heat being moderated, as in the West Indies, by the cool sea-breezes. The native population is not inclined to severe agricultural labour, and to carry on the industries of the islands it has been found necessary to import labourers from other parts of Polynesia and from India.

FIG. 21.—A FIJIAN.

The Fiji islanders present one of the most striking examples to be found in the Empire of a whole population which has been induced by the efforts of Christian missionaries to abandon cannibalism and other savage vices and to adopt a peaceable and comparatively civilised life.

The trade of the islands has greatly increased since their annexation to the Empire.

The capital of the islands is Suva, in the island of Viti Levu.

The Odds and Ends of the Empire.

A few small and isolated possessions of the Empire in the Pacific still remain to be mentioned.

Pitcairn Island, about two miles long and three-quarters of a mile wide, lies in the Pacific about midway between Australia and America. Its inhabitants are the descendants of mutineers from the English man-of-war *Bounty*, who settled here more than a hundred years ago, and married native wives from other islands. The little patch of ground on which they lived was found insufficient for the growing population, and a few years ago the greater number of the people were transferred to Norfolk Island.

Norfolk Island was once used as a convict station to which the worst criminals were sent from New South Wales. When the penal settlement was broken up, in 1853, the Pitcairn Islanders were allowed to settle there, and they have maintained the simple and primitive life to which they were accustomed. A missionary school is also supported in the island, to which native children from the Melanesian islands are brought for instruction by English clergymen. The area of the whole group of islands, of which Norfolk Island is the chief, is only twelve square miles.

The Cook Islands were taken under British protection in 1888, at the request of the people themselves. A considerable trade is carried on with New Zealand, to which the islands send cotton, coffee, copra, and tobacco. The largest island, Raro-tonga, is an important mission centre of the Wesleyan Church, which here maintains an institution for the education of native missionaries.

Should a Panama canal ever be completed, this group would become of importance as a station for coal and supplies between Australasia and Central America.

We need not expect that in these Pacific islands there will ever be a large population of British people. The climate of the Torrid Zone is seldom favourable for the European races. We shall have to point out this more particularly when we speak of the lands under the British flag in India, in parts of Africa, and even in the most northern districts of Australia. English people go to them to trade, to direct native labour, to govern, but they do not go to them in large numbers to form permanent homes.

***

CHAPTER VII.

AUSTRALASIA—NEW ZEALAND.

The South Temperate Zone.

As we go southward through the Pacific, we find ourselves passing out of the heat of the Torrid Zone, and coming once again into a cooler climate. We are in the **South Temperate Zone.**

Observe that there is much less land in the half of the globe which is south of the Equator than in the half which is north of it. The continents become narrower and the oceans wider as they extend southward. Notice also that of the lands which are in the South Temperate Zone, **Australia, New Zealand, Tasmania,** and **South Africa** are either entirely or chiefly under the British flag. We may therefore say that, with the exception of South

America, all the best regions of the South Temperate Zone are possessed and inhabited mainly by British people.

New Zealand.

New Zealand, the first great colony to which we come, is often called "The Britain of the South." It has many points of resemblance to our own islands which make it deserve this name.

First among these is its maritime position. It stands out in the sea at some distance from the neighbouring continent, and has a coast indented with many good harbours.

Like this country, again, it consists mainly of two large islands, and these islands are only about one-sixth less in size than those which make up the United Kingdom.

FIG. 25.—NEW ZEALAND.

Northern New Zealand is warmer than any part of this country, but on the whole the climate is more like our own than is that of any other large colony in which British people have settled.

The chief productions of both countries are very similar. On account of the temperate climate and the moist atmosphere given by the surrounding sea, most of the plants and animals of the British Islands flourish when carried over to New Zealand.

It is a singular fact that when the country was discovered it contained no animal, wild or tame, which might serve as human food. Pigs were introduced by Captain Cook, and soon became scattered in large numbers over the country in a wild state. Great care has been taken by the colonists to introduce not merely such domestic animals as the horse, cow, and sheep, but also many which serve as game, such as the deer, hare, and rabbit, together with many European birds and fishes. British plants, fruits, and flowers have in the same way been brought over. The result is that now the English traveller or emigrant sees around him most of the common objects to which he is accustomed at home.

A Second England.

Even in the scenery, with many differences, there are also striking resemblances. About this a well-known writer has said :—

" In New Zealand everything is English. The scenery, the colour and general appearance of the water, and the shape of the hills are very much like that with which we are familiar in the West of Ireland and the Highlands of Scotland. The mountains are brown and sharp and serrated, the rivers are bright and rapid, and the lakes are deep and blue and bosomed among the mountains. If a long-sleeping Briton could be set among the Otago hills and told on waking that he was travelling in Galway or in the West of Scotland, he might easily be deceived, though he knew those countries well."

Besides these points of similarity it may be added that the settlers themselves have consisted more entirely of English, Scottish, and Irish people, and have had a less admixture of foreign races than is the case in any other of the great colonies.

We can now understand why New Zealand is sometimes spoken of as "The Britain of the South." There is no part of the world to which an Englishman could go where things around would so often remind him of home.

The History of New Zealand.

We may now speak very briefly of the history of New Zealand. It was discovered in 1642 by the Dutch, who gave it the name it now bears, but made no settlement. After this nothing more is heard of it for more than a century, but between 1769 and 1778 it was visited by the famous English navigator Captain Cook, who explored the coasts and described the country very accurately, as well as the native inhabitants, who were a fierce race of cannibals. Whalers, traders, and others after this visited the islands from time to time, but the first actual settlement was made by English missionaries in the North Island in 1814.

Twenty-five years later, in 1839, colonisation began in good earnest, and under the direction of different companies large numbers of emigrants were sent out. In

1810 New Zealand was made a separate colony, and in the same year a treaty was made with the native chiefs by which the sovereignty of the North Island was ceded to Britain, but the right of selling their lands was reserved to the natives. A few years later war broke out with the Maories, as the natives were called, and this contest was not concluded till 1869, since which time the colony has enjoyed peace. In a little more than fifty years a country which was inhabited only by savage tribes whose greatest delight was in warfare, and whose constant practice was to eat those whom they had killed or captured in battle, has become the home of more than 750,000 British people, enjoying the comforts and advantages of civilised life just as people do in England.

The Maories.

There are still over 40,000 Maories in New Zealand. They are now a peaceable people, who have given up many of their savage customs, and who either cultivate their own lands or work as farmers, shepherds, or sailors for English employers. Some of the tribes have a large income from the lands they sell or lease to English settlers. Great numbers have been converted to Christianity, and they have schools, churches, and clergymen of their own. They also elect men of their own race to be members of the Legislature of the colony and so assist in making the laws.

Facts about New Zealand.

Of the two large islands which make up the greater part of New Zealand one is called the North Island and

the other the Middle or South Island. Stewart Island is
sometimes called the South Island; it is small and not
important. The strait which separates the two larger
islands is only a few miles wide at its narrowest part.

From north to south New Zealand extends about 1,100

FIG. 26.—MOUNT COOK.

miles. Its greatest breadth is a little over 150 miles. It
stands far out in the Pacific, 1,200 miles from Australia,
the nearest continent.

New Zealand is a mountainous country. The low
mountain ranges in the North Island are from 1,500 to
4,000 feet high, with a few volcanic peaks of still greater
height. Along the whole of the West Coast of the Middle
Island runs a range called the **Southern Alps**, the higher

summits of which are covered with perpetual snow. The height of **Mount Cook**, the loftiest peak, is 12,348 feet. Upon Mount Cook, as well as at other points along the Southern Alps, glaciers of immense size are found.

Many of the mountain-peaks in the North Island are extinct volcanoes, and there can still be seen at their summits the hollow craters from which issued fire and lava. Two or three of the volcanic mountains still show signs of activity, and slight earthquake shocks are sometimes felt throughout the whole island.

In 1886 a violent eruption took place in what is known as the Hot Lake District of the North Island. The famous pink and white terraces formed by these hot lakes, which had long been considered among the most wonderful and beautiful sights in nature, were destroyed by this eruption.

While mountains are a striking feature in the scenery of parts of New Zealand, there are also extensive plains, with much undulating country, and fertile valleys among the hills. The **Canterbury Plains**, on the Middle Island, stretch for more than 100 miles along the East Coast in an almost unbroken level.

New Zealand is a pastoral, farming, and mining country, and from its pastures, farms, and mines it produces much to export to other lands. Although the most distant of our colonies, a very large part of all that New Zealand thus has to part with is sent to the United Kingdom. It is well to learn about these exports, for they help us to understand what are the occupations of the people.

New Zealand Mutton.

In our cities and towns we often observe " New Zealand mutton " advertised or exposed for sale in butchers' shops. If we inquire we shall probably find that this mutton costs less than English mutton. Why is it that this mutton can be sold more cheaply than our own, and in what way does it get to this country ?

In the greater part of New Zealand the climate is so mild that sheep feed in the pastures all the year round, and require no barns to shelter them in winter. They are also kept in vast numbers, a single owner often having from 20,000 to 100,000 sheep, the whole taken care of by a few men. These circumstances greatly diminish the cost of rearing them. So from its fertile and well-watered pastures New Zealand can always send away excellent mutton at a very cheap rate.

But for a long time it seemed impossible to send it to England, where it was most needed. A few years ago, however, it was found that mutton could be sent from New Zealand to Great Britain in a frozen state. Since then the trade has grown so rapidly that now every year above a million and a half of frozen carcases of sheep reach this country from New Zealand.*

Great care is used by the New Zealand farmers in securing good breeds of sheep for the mutton which is to be sent to the English market. When the animals are in perfect condition they are taken from the paddocks where they have been reared and fattened to the freezing estab-

* In 1902 the value of the frozen meat exported to Great Britain amounted to £3,218,729.

lishment, which is usually built beside the sea-coast, so
as to be near the place of shipment. A visit to one of
these establishments shows us the whole process of
preparation.

The sheep are first skilfully slaughtered, skinned, and
dressed ready for market, great attention being paid to perfect cleanliness. After being hung up for some hours to
cool, the carcases are transferred to the freezing-chamber.
This is a large room, provided with thick walls and heavy
doors completely excluding light and heat.

A visitor sometimes gets permission to see the interior
of a freezing-chamber. However warm the air may be
out of doors, he should take care to be provided with a
heavy great-coat. An attendant, carrying a lantern, un-
locks one of the doors, and carefully closes it after entering.
Inside the temperature is found to be like that of the Arctic
regions. The breath which comes from the mouth is condensed into thick vapour. Suspended just as we see them
in butchers' shops are thousands of carcases of mutton, but
if touched they are found to be almost as hard as marble.
In this condition they are to remain until they reach
England. Curiosity is soon satisfied in the atmosphere of
a freezing-chamber, and so in a few minutes the visitor is
glad to get back into the open air.*

---

* The extreme cold of the freezing chamber is produced by a process
which has been described as follows :—

"Air, at the ordinary natural temperature is compressed to say one-
third of its natural bulk by steam power. It is then let into a chamber
with walls impervious to heat. The sudden expansion of the air to its
natural bulk again reduces it to one-third of its former temperature, producing an intense cold within the chamber: and this process being

I

Each carcase, when frozen, is encased in a clean white calico bag, and taken from the freezing-chamber to a similar one in the hold of one of the large steamships which carry the mutton to England. A single vessel often carries 30,000 or 40,000 carcases, landing them in London in the same state in which they left the works in New Zealand. At the London Docks they are stored once more in freezing chambers, and thence distributed day by day to different parts of the country.

The sheep thus sent to us are a very small part of those reared in the country, which number already sixteen or seventeen millions. The wool of these is sent to the United Kingdom year after year, and forms an export even more valuable than that of mutton.

Other New Zealand Products.

Besides mutton New Zealand supplies us with other articles of food, such as **beef**, both frozen and preserved in tins, **wheat, dairy butter,** and **fruit**. It also sends a great many farm and dairy products to Australia. New Zealand never suffers from drought, as Australia sometimes does. So when the crops of grain and vegetables have failed in New South Wales or Queensland, New Zealanders are able to send them all they require.

A peculiar product of the country is **New Zealand flax.** The plant is one which grows wild in swamps or marshy places, and has a leaf shaped like that of the common iris,

constantly maintained by steam power, the temperature within the chamber is permanently kept down to a point corresponding to the compression of the air."

but from four to eight feet long. From this leaf a strong fibre is obtained, which is exported to England and other countries and used in rope-making.

Kauri gum is another singular product of New Zealand which forms an important article of commerce. It comes from a pine tree, forests of which still extend over the northern parts of the North Island. But the best quality and far the largest quantity of gum is dug from beneath the earth, where it has been hidden for centuries after dropping from forests which have long since disappeared.

Kauri gum closely resembles amber, and it is much used in Great Britain and America for making the best and most expensive kinds of varnish. It is found over a large extent of country, and in digging for it a good many people get employment. The only implements which the gum-digger requires are a long steel rod and a shovel. The former he thrusts here and there into the ground until he touches a piece of gum, which practice enables him to distinguish from any other substance. This he then proceeds to dig out. Sometimes the gum is in small lumps, sometimes in pieces that weigh a hundredweight.

Though finding it in the way I have described seems so much a matter of chance, large quantities are procured, and more than £300,000 worth is sometimes exported in a single year.

Gold in New Zealand.

Gold-mining is an important industry in New Zealand, as shown by the fact that about £50,000,000 worth has been obtained since it was first discovered about thirty

years ago. The gold is found in many parts of the islands,·
and under very different circumstances: sometimes in the
beds of streams or among the sands of the sea-shore, from
which it is obtained by washing ; or embedded in quartz
and other rocks, from which it has to be crushed by
powerful and expensive machinery.

Gold-mining in New Zealand is not now an employment which excites people with the hope of making a fortune
in a short time, but has become a regular industry, often
requiring a large amount of capital to carry it on, and in
which men earn regular wages as in other kinds of work.
Gold is still sent to England every year to the value of
nearly a million pounds sterling.

Towns and Harbours of New Zealand.

Wellington is the capital of New Zealand. **Auckland,
Christchurch,** and **Dunedin** are other important towns.
Lyttelton (the port of Christchurch), Wellington, Auckland, and Dunedin have all excellent harbours, which
are already defended by batteries of artillery, and might
be made very strong. At Auckland and Lyttelton fine
docks have been built at great expense, in which our
ships of war, even of the largest size, or trading vessels
can be repaired. A wonderful advantage it is to a
great naval Power and trading nation such as ours thus
to have docks and harbours at the other side of the
world. No other European nation has anything of the
kind.

A telegraph cable connects New Zealand with Australia,
whence the line is continued to England ; so every day

our people in New Zealand read in their papers about what
is taking place in this country.

From Auckland in the north, Dunedin in the south,
and Wellington midway between them, steamship lines

FIG. 27.—TE ARO, A SUBURB OF WELLINGTON.
(*From a Photograph by Burton Bros., Dunedin.*)

run to Australia or Tasmania. We shall take the southern
route, passing round "The Bluff," which is the southern
point of the Middle Island. As we sail away westward
and look back upon New Zealand we feel that this
"Britain of the South" is one of the most beautiful
homes that our race has found anywhere in the world—a
land which can support many millions of British people,

producing everything to make them prosperous, comfortable, and happy.   After four or five days' steaming we reach **Hobart** in **Tasmania**.

---◆◆◆---

CHAPTER VIII.

AUSTRALASIA—TASMANIA

Tasmania.

THE island of **Tasmania** lies off the southern extremity of Australia, from which it is separated by the **Bass Straits**, at their narrowest part 200 miles wide.   The area of the island is 26,215 square miles, and it is therefore about five-sixths the size of Ireland.   The climate is very fine and well suited to Europeans.   Being much cooler than the neighbouring continent, Tasmania has become a favourite summer resort for Australians.   The island is settled chiefly on the northern, eastern, and south-eastern coasts.   The western side is largely covered with dense forest, or an almost impenetrable scrub, which makes it unfit for agriculture and difficult to explore.   Late discoveries have proved this part of the country to be very rich in mineral deposits.   The surface of the island is generally hilly or mountainous, and numerous streams flow down from the higher ground to water the fertile valleys.

The island was discovered in 1642 by **Tasman**, a Dutch navigator, from whom its present name is derived.   He himself called it **Van Diemen's Land**, the name by which it was long known.   The first settlement was not made till 1803, when it was occupied by Britain as a penal colony.

Attracted by the fine climate and soil, many settlers of
wealth and education soon came to the colony, availing
themselves of the labour of convicts in carrying on their
agricultural and pastoral pursuits. The convict system
was abolished in 1853.

The population now numbers about 172,000. The
native race has become quite extinct, the last native having
died in 1876.

One of the important industries of Tasmania is fruit
culture.

Tasmanian Fruit in England.

At Covent Garden, the great fruit and vegetable
market of London, during the months of April, May, or
June, we may often see large quantities of beautiful, fresh-
looking apples being sold by auction, and we may be told
that it is only five or six weeks since they were picked
from the trees. It is plain that they could not have been
grown in England, but must have come from the other
side of the world, where the seasons are the opposite of
our own.

These apples come from Tasmania, and reach us at a
time when our own apple trees are only beginning to bud
and flower, and when fresh fruit is, therefore, most accept-
able. Tasmania, in soil and climate, is probably better
suited than any other part of the Empire to produce our
common English fruits. Not only apples, but pears,
apricots, currants, gooseberries, raspberries, and straw-
berries grow in profusion. Until a few years ago the
chief difficulty of fruit-growers in Tasmania was to find a
market for their abundant fruit. A great deal was made

into jam, and sent away in that state.   But if fresh fruit was sent to England, it was spoiled by the heat of the torrid regions through which it had to pass.   At last, however, just as New Zealanders discovered that mutton could be sent safely when stored in freezing chambers on the steam-ships, so Tasmanians found that apples could be landed in London in a sound condition if sent in chambers kept constantly cool.   So now the Tasmanians, from their orchards more than 12,000 miles away, supply us with apples at a season when we have none of our own, and cannot get them from colonies like Canada, which only send fruit to us in the autumn of the Northern Hemisphere.

In the best Tasmanian orchards much skill is shown in the cultivation of fruit.   The orchards are constantly tilled, and kept free from weeds throughout the year; water is often brought in channels from a considerable distance to irrigate the soil; the trees, as they grow, are carefully pruned in such a way as to admit the light and air to all parts, and thus bring all the fruit to perfection. There are few pleasanter sights than that which a Tas-manian orchard of fifty or a hundred acres presents in the month of March or April, when every tree is laden with the rosy, russet, or golden fruit.   From the orchard the fruit is taken to an apple store-house, where many thousands of bushels may sometimes be seen together, sorted into separate bins according to their variety and quality.   At the store-houses they are carefully packed in cases holding a bushel each, and are then shipped away to Australia or England.

Other Tasmanian Products.

The fruit of Tasmania has first been mentioned, not because it is the most important product of the colony, but because it is one that is likely to increase greatly under this new system of carriage, and because the trade in it illustrates in an interesting way the closeness of our connection with the most remote parts of the Empire.

Wool is the largest export of Tasmania, as it is of Australia and New Zealand. The climate has been found particularly favourable for carrying on experiments in breeding superior kinds of sheep, with a view to improving the quality of the wool. It is doubtful whether better sheep can be found anywhere else in the world. They command high prices in the Australian colonies, and several hundred guineas have sometimes been paid for a single Tasmanian sheep.

Gold is found in considerable quantities, and some newly discovered silver mines at **Mount Zeehan** promise to be very productive. At **Mount Bischoff** is one of the most valuable **tin** mines in the world. About £100,000 worth of this metal alone is shipped every year to England and America. There are also several coal mines.

A traveller often finds out much about the productions and exports of a new country from what he observes as he passes over its railways. If you were travelling thus through the northern parts of Tasmania in the autumn you would probably see tens of thousands of well-filled sacks piled up at the stations. The sacks contain potatoes, for which the soil is peculiarly adapted, and which the island supplies in large quantities to Australia along with other vegetables and fruit. At other stations you would see large piles of the bark of the **Wattle Tree**. This bark is very valuable for tanning, and a great deal of it is sent every year to England. Tasmania has large forests of fine timber, and some of its many beautiful woods are particularly good for cabinet-work, for which purpose they are exported to this country.

A cable gives Tasmania telegraphic communication with Australia and the rest of the world.

Hobart in the south and **Launceston** in the north are the two chief towns. From both of them steamships run to Australia, with which Tasmania has now become confederated. A voyage of 200 miles takes us across the Bass Straits to Australia.

CHAPTER IX.

THE AUSTRALIAN CONTINENT—NEW SOUTH WALES.

Australia.

WE have now come in the Southern Hemisphere to a portion of the Empire which in size is only second to the Dominion of Canada. You see on the map that **Australia** is an immense island, by far the largest in the world. It is, perhaps, more correctly spoken of as a continent. From east to west, at its widest point, it extends 2,400 miles, and from north to south 1,970 miles. The length of its coast-line is about 8,000 miles. The area of its whole surface is more than three millions of square miles.

Australia is, therefore, nearly as large as the whole of

Europe. It is about twenty-five times the size of the United Kingdom.

The whole of this vast area is under the British flag, and is gradually being occupied by an English-speaking people.

The French were before us in Canada, the Dutch in South Africa, the Spaniards in the West Indies, while in India we had to compete with Portuguese, Dutch, and French. Our possessions in these different countries were therefore gained partly by conquest and partly by settlement. In Australasia alone no other European nation had tried to get a footing before ourselves. Our people have thus been left free to occupy and settle their different colonies without interference.

First Settlement of Australia.

When men or women are convicted of crimes they are often sent to gaol, or, if the offence is a serious one, to convict prisons, where they are closely watched and made to labour, sometimes for many years, sometimes through the whole course of their lives. For this purpose almost every town has a gaol, and at places like Dartmoor and Chatham, large prisons are maintained where hundreds of criminals are guarded and employed.

Many years ago it was believed that one of the best ways to deal with people who had broken the laws was to send them away to some new and distant land. This was partly as a punishment, partly that their labour might be usefully employed, and partly in the hope that if they wished to amend, they might in a new country more

easily get a fresh start in life. Criminals had thus been
sent out to the West Indies, and to Virginia and the Caro-
linas in America, but after the American Revolutionary
war it was found necessary to fix upon some new place,
and the far distant and then quite unsettled Australia was
chosen.

No doubt those who carried out this plan thought it
was for the best, and so long as a colony had no other
population than the convicts there was nothing wrong in
it. But when free settlers began to flock into the country
they soon raised objections to the new colonies being
burdened with so many bad citizens, and English people
had to admit that their view was just. **Transportation**
was therefore abolished, after it had been carried on for
nearly fifty years. It had served a useful purpose in
making known an entirely unsettled land to which emigration had not yet been turned, and in overcoming the first
great difficulties of settlement.

Canada and Australia Compared.

We have seen that Australia, the largest division of
the Empire in the Southern Hemisphere, is nearly equal in
size to Canada, the greatest in the Northern. In other
ways, however, the contrast between these two great
countries is very remarkable.

Let us compare them briefly, that we may understand
the different circumstances in which our people find
themselves when they settle in these widely separate
parts of the Empire.

Both comprise immense regions where millions of

British people are finding comfortable and prosperous homes, though in Canada they must be prepared to endure a greater degree of winter cold, in Australia a greater intensity of summer heat, than in these islands.

In Canada we are struck with the extraordinary abundance of water, opening up the country in every direction. Broad lakes and splendid rivers stretch across the continent, with ponds and gurgling brooks and rivulets everywhere.

One of the most marked features, on the other hand, of Australia is the absence of large rivers and lakes to give the means of inland navigation, or even to furnish sufficient supplies of fresh water.

The portions of Northern Canada which stretch up to the Arctic Circle are made uninhabitable by the excessive cold.

Northern Australia, on the contrary, extends into the Torrid Zone, and the parts which are uninhabitable are made so by excessive heat.

In parts of Canada the farmer sometimes has to dread an early frost ; in Australia he must guard against the chance of droughts which destroy alike his crops and cattle.

These are only a few illustrations which will show us that people who go to Canada have to get into different ways of life from those who go to Australia.

In both countries there are difficulties to contend with. But we must always remember that it is by overcoming difficulties that both men and nations become strong and self-reliant.

The Southern Cross.

When we are sailing southwards shortly after crossing the Equator, a new constellation will appear in the southern sky, a constellation never seen by those who live in the

FIG. 28.—THE SOUTHERN CROSS.

Northern Hemisphere. As we get further south this constellation will appear higher in the heavens, always pointing to the South Pole, as our Great Bear in the Northern Hemisphere points to the North Pole. The arrangement of the stars in this constellation is shown in the picture which is given above. It is known as the **Southern Cross,** and the Australians have taken it as an emblem of their great island. The stars of the Southern

Cross may be seen, together with the **Union Jack**, upon the flags of New South Wales and Victoria.

Divisions of Australia.

Australia is divided into five provinces or states: **New South Wales, Victoria, Queensland, South Australia,** and **Western Australia.** Up to the year 1901 there had been no common Government for the whole Australian continent. Each colony had acted independently of all the others, with a Legislature and a governor of its own.

But by Act of the Imperial Parliament, and consent of all the colonies, the whole of Australia, together with Tasmania, became, on the first day of the Twentieth Century (January 1st, 1901), confederated under the name of THE COMMONWEALTH OF AUSTRALIA, into a single State, having one central Parliament, and a Governor-General, as in Canada. We may be sure that under this new form of government, the Colonies will become even more powerful and important parts of the Empire than before.

We may now say something about each Colony separately.

New South Wales.

New South Wales received its name in 1770 from Captain Cook, who explored its coasts, and it originally included the whole Eastern side of the continent. **Victoria** was separated from it in 1851, and **Queensland** in 1859. The territory which it still retains, however, is so extensive that the area of the colony is six times that of England.

The first settlement was made in 1788. On the 20th
of January in that year **Captain Philip**, who had been
sent out to form a penal colony, landed on the shores of
Port Jackson, and proclaimed British supremacy over
Australia.

The great difficulties which were met with in forming
the first settlement were gradually overcome, and so many
free immigrants had come into the country during the
first fifty years that further transportation was objected
to. It was entirely abolished in 1853, and in 1856 the
same complete self-government was granted to the colony
which the Canadian provinces had received some years
before.

Sydney.

Around the spot where Captain Philip landed now
stands the capital of the colony, **Sydney**, which in little
more than a hundred years has grown to be a city with
upwards of 496,000 inhabitants, while the population of
the whole colony, though it has been twice subdivided by
setting off the Colonies of Victoria and Queensland, is
now about 1,350,000.

Sydney is situated upon one of the largest and most
beautiful harbours in the world. But we have before
learned that it requires something more than a fine harbour
to make a great and wealthy commercial port such as
Sydney is. We observed that Liverpool was a great
commercial port because it had behind it large manufacturing cities with millions of inhabitants who had to be
supplied with food and the materials used in manufacture.
Now Sydney and other Australian cities have become

great because they have behind them a vast country which produces this food and material for manufacture to be exported to other countries, and most of all to England.

We may illustrate this by describing the greatest industry of Australia, that of rearing sheep. In this, New South Wales has always taken the lead. It is the great pastoral colony, and has now within its borders nearly 56,000,000 sheep.

Australian Wool.

The woollen mills in different parts of England, and especially in Yorkshire, give employment to many hundred thousands of workmen. The cloth which these mills produce is not only used to clothe our own people here, but is sent to every part of the world, and has become one of the chief articles of our commerce.

But the United Kingdom itself produces only a small proportion of all the wool which we thus manufacture into cloth. To buy enough to keep our mills and workmen busy we sometimes spend as much as £25,000,000 in a single year. It is brought from many lands, but by far the greater portion of what we use comes from other parts of our own Empire. The largest supplies of all we get from Australia and the neighbouring colonies of New Zealand and Tasmania.

Although Australia has been settled by British people little more than a hundred years, it has already become **the largest wool-exporting country of the world.** Sheep were first brought from England about the year 1800, and now there are 96,000,000 in Australia alone, and in the whole of Australasia more than 115,000,000.

J

Nearly all the wool from these vast flocks comes to England, and of all that comes a great deal is sent to supply the mills of Yorkshire. Thus the industry of those who are spinning, weaving, and dyeing wool in this country is very closely connected with the industry of those who are producing it at the other side of the world.

The remarkably rapid increase of the flocks to which we have referred is due to the fact that Australia has great advantages as a pastoral country. The climate is so mild that it is unnecessary to provide barns or other shelter for sheep in winter. As there is no snow, the pastures supply them with food all the year round. There are vast regions of country unfit for agriculture, and scantily covered with wild grasses and shrubs, on which sheep are found to thrive. Large flocks are kept even where the vegetation is so scanty that from five to ten acres of land are allowed for each sheep. Under such circumstances, if the flock is large, the estate on which it feeds must be immense.

Sheep Runs and Squatters.

An estate of this kind is called a " Sheep Run," and the proprietor, who may either own the land or lease it from Government, is called a "Squatter." A single squatter often owns from 10,000 to 250,000 sheep. The size of the run depends partly upon the number of sheep to be pastured, and partly upon the character of the vegetation. Where the latter is scanty and the flocks large, the run may cover hundreds of thousands of acres. Even for such estates as this there is plenty of room in

Australia. In New South Wales alone about 150,000,000 acres of land are held on lease from the Government, besides what has been sold.

Formerly the flocks roamed at large over the open

FIG. 29.—ON A SHEEP RUN.

country, tended by shepherds who lived a rough life in rude huts. Now on the large runs the "station," as the house of the squatter is called, is usually a comfortable and sometimes a luxurious home, fitted with everything commonly found in a well-furnished house in England. The

run itself is enclosed and divided into paddocks by wire
fences. The shepherds are "Boundary Riders," mounted
men who spend the whole day in the saddle, riding from
place to place to visit the flocks.

The Squatter's Enemies.

Great as are Australia's advantages for rearing sheep,
the squatter has often great difficulties and dangers with
which to contend. That which he fears most of all is
drought. Sometimes for months together there is no rain,
the grass dies, and the only food the sheep can get is that
furnished by the desert shrubs which even severe drought
cannot kill. Still worse, the springs and water-courses
dry up, and then there have been times when thousands
and even millions of sheep have died in a single season
from want of water.

Occasionally, after a prolonged drought, the rains
descend in torrents, the beds of the shallow rivers over-
flow, and floods cover the low country for miles around.

With one strange enemy the squatter often has a
desperate fight. In this country we only know the rabbit
as an inoffensive little animal, which is allowed to burrow
in parks and hedges, and when shot is used for food. In
Australia rabbits have become a terrible pest, swarming
over the country in millions, and ruining whole runs by
eating up the grass on which the sheep feed. Great
numbers of people are employed and thousands of pounds
are spent in shooting, trapping, poisoning, and in many
other ways destroying them. Hundreds of miles of fine
wire fence are sometimes constructed to cut them off from

certain districts. But a considerable article of commerce is derived even from this nuisance. Many millions of rabbit-skins are every year sent to England, where they are employed for making the felt used in the manufacture of hats, and for other purposes.

New South Wales has many other industries besides that of producing wool. Large herds of **cattle** are reared, **orange groves** cover many thousands of acres, and **fruit-growing** is constantly becoming a more important occupation. In some districts the agricultural lands are excellent. The **coal** mines give employment to many thousands of miners, and coal is exported not only to the other colonies, but to America, China, and South Africa. There are valuable mines of **gold, silver, copper, tin,** and **antimony.**

CHAPTER X.

THE AUSTRALIAN CONTINENT—VICTORIA.

Victoria.

Victoria, as we see on the map, is in the southern part of Australia, and it therefore has a climate which is cooler and more agreeable for Europeans than that of any other portion of the continent.

It has an area of nearly 88,000 square miles, and is about equal in size to England, Wales, and Scotland. Although the smallest of the Australian colonies, it is one of the most wealthy and important.

The resources of Victoria are varied. As in New South Wales, a great many sheep and cattle are reared.

but the tendency in late years has been to devote the land to agriculture, for which the cooler climate and less exposure to drought make the colony well suited. Increasing attention is also being given to vine-growing, and the production of wine is now more than a million

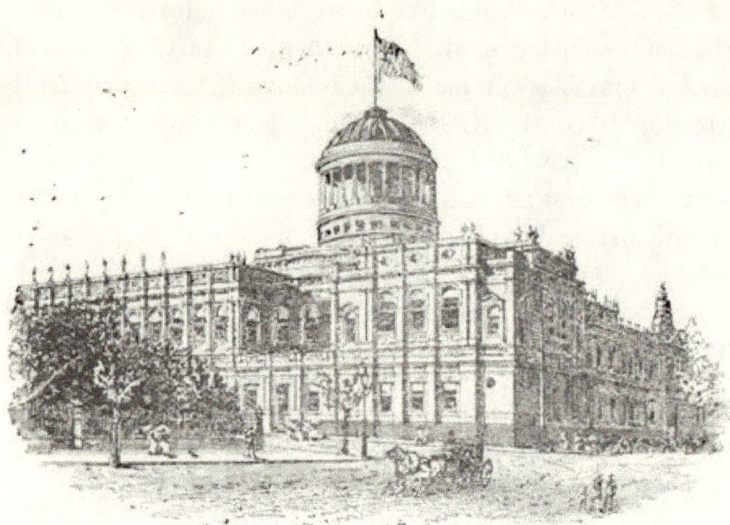

FIG. 39.—NEW LAW COURTS, MELBOURNE.
(*From a Photograph by Mr. Lieit, Melbourne.*)

and a half gallons each year.   Manufactures of various kinds are largely carried on in Melbourne and the smaller towns of the colony.

But it is neither for its wool nor its wheat, its wine nor its manufactures, that Victoria has been most celebrated in the past.

Sixty years ago **Melbourne**, now the capital of the colony, was a small village with a few hundreds of inhabitants. Now it is a city containing nearly 500,000 people, and so is one of the great cities of the Empire. This is a very wonderful change to take place in so short a time, and it is interesting to know how it came about.

Gold.

In the year 1851 Victoria was separated from New South Wales, and formed into an independent colony. Up to this time its population had grown slowly and steadily, as settlers came to take up land in districts favourable for farming or for establishing sheep runs. But in that year an event occurred which suddenly drew to it people from all parts of the globe, and made the colony more thought of and talked about for a time throughout the civilised world than almost any other place. The **discovery of gold** was the event which caused this great change in the fortunes of the country. At many points within sixty or seventy miles of Melbourne the precious metal was found scattered through the soil and gravel in the beds of streams, along the valleys, or on the slopes of the hills. Deposits so rich had never been found before. Sometimes a lucky miner would light upon a " nugget," as the lumps of gold were called, worth several hundreds or even several thousands of pounds.

The Rush to the " Diggings."

The excitement caused by these discoveries was very great. Men hurried in thousands from every part of the neighbouring colonies to the gold-fields. In the cities lawyers and doctors gave up their professions, and mer-

chants and clerks abandoned their offices to betake themselves to mining. The ships in the harbours were left
without sailors, the streets without policemen, the gaols
without warders. The news spread to Europe and America,
and soon enterprising men of all nations began pouring
into the country by thousands. The arrivals during the
year 1852 alone numbered 100,000, so that the population
of the colony was doubled. In that year one hundred and
seventy-four tons of gold, valued at £14,000,000, were
taken from the ground. Within ten years £100,000,000
worth of gold had been sent away from Victoria.

With such vast numbers of men joining in the search
for gold, while a few got rich by mining many met with
disappointment. Fortunately the gold "rush" caused a
demand for almost every kind of labour. The hundreds of
thousands of people crowding into the country had to be
supplied with shelter, food, clothing, and other necessaries
of life. Farmers and shepherds got good prices for their
grain and vegetables, sheep and cattle; the harbour was
full of ships bringing manufactured goods from England;
miles of streets were being built up with warehouses, shops,
dwellings, and public buildings, and so everybody had
plenty of employment.

There is an old fable which tells us of a farmer who,
when dying, told his sons that there was a treasure con-
cealed in a certain field of their farm. After their father
was dead and buried the sons set to work searching for
this treasure, digging carefully over every foot of the
ground. After long search, being unable to find the
treasure, they again went back to the farming. Then it

was that they found out the real meaning of what their
father had said, for the field had been tilled so thoroughly
that it produced crops and gave them a return such as it
had never done before.

Something like this happens in countries like Victoria
when gold is discovered. People rush there to search for
treasure, but in doing this they find out the lands which
are suited for farms or vineyards, orchards or pastures, and
when the treasure is exhausted they stay to work at those
quiet but permanent employments which best build up a
country.

On the very fields where thousands of miners once
camped may now be seen beautiful towns surrounded
by fertile farms. Melbourne, which grew rich through
gold, is now kept rich by the wool and cattle, wheat and
wine, which are raised in these great farming districts.

Gold-mining at the Present Day.

A good deal of gold is, however, still obtained.
When the richer mines had become exhausted, and all
the gold had been washed from the surface soil, shafts,
sometimes nearly 2,000 feet deep, were sunk to reefs of
quartz beneath. The rock, when brought to the surface,
is crushed by powerful machinery to a fine powder, from
which the gold is extracted by various processes.

The period of gold excitement in the history of Victoria
enables us to understand how the discovery of mines
sometimes makes rapid changes in a few years, turning a
small town into a great city, or lifting an unimportant
colony into the position of an influential State. We

find that the same change has taken place, or is still going on, in other countries occupied by our people.

We have mentioned the immense amount of gold that has been obtained in Victoria. Smaller but still very

FIG. 31.— GOLD-CRUSHING " STAMPS."

considerable quantities are dug up in the other **Australasian** colonies. Altogether its value has amounted to more than £300,000,000. Of all this vast sum, by far the greatest part has come to England.

If we look into the jewellers' and goldsmiths' shops as we walk along the streets of any large town we see at once how much gold is used in this country in making plate, watches, and jewellery of many kinds.

A great deal is used in various arts. The manufacture of gold in many forms gives employment to a large number of our people.

Still more is required for money. Many millions of sovereigns and half-sovereigns are constantly circulating from hand to hand in carrying on trade and industry, or are stored up in the banks ready for use.

Sometimes the gold of Australia is sent to England in the form of bars or ingots, which are sold here to be coined into money at the Royal Mint, or used in manufactures. But a great deal also comes in the form of money itself.

A great many of the sovereigns used in this country are not merely made of Australian gold, but are actually coined in Australia. If you have an opportunity to look carefully over a number of sovereigns, you will probably discover among them some which have the letter M or the letter S stamped upon them just beneath the profile of Queen Victoria. The M shows that the sovereign which bears it was coined at Melbourne; S is the mark of the Sydney Mint in New South Wales. At these two branches of the Royal Mint more than four millions of sovereigns are often coined in a single year. A large proportion of these are sent to England, and in some years more than three millions have been received in the Bank of England, from which they pass again into general circulation in this country.

Observe that these Australian sovereigns, though made

on the other side of the world, bear the stamp of Queen
Victoria's or King Edward's head, and so are taken everywhere as English Currency, and indeed can only be distinguished from coins made in England by the marks
referred to, so slight that few observe them or understand
what they mean.

Australian Naval Defence.

With all these treasures to guard, it is not wonderful
that the people of Sydney and Melbourne should take
pains to keep safe what they have got, and we need not
therefore be surprised to find that both cities are strongly
fortified against attack.

While she is strengthening herself within, Australia
has not forgotten to protect herself from enemies without.
Unluckily, perhaps, Australia has neighbours who are not
of British origin, for Germany, France, and Holland have
now got possessions in the South Pacific.   In order, therefore, to be safe against any attack, and also to be able to
help to defend the Empire in case of war, the Australians
have arranged with the British Government for the supply
of a certain number of ships of war which will be
kept usually in Australian waters.   The cost of keeping
up these ships is paid for by the Governments of the
Australian colonies.   The vessels have been specially built
for the purpose, and have been called by Australian names,
such as the *Ringarooma, Mildura, Boomerang, Karakatta,*
and so on.   They are fast and well-armed ships, and may
be depended upon to do honour to the flag which they
carry, and which is the white ensign of the Royal Navy.
The picture shows us one of the largest of the Australian

FIG. 32.—H.M.S. RINGAROOMA.

(From a Photograph by Messrs. Symonds & Co., Portsmouth.)

squadron, the *Ringarooma*. She has a speed of sixteen knots an hour, and carries eight guns.

CHAPTER XI.

THE AUSTRALIAN CONTINENT—SOUTH AUSTRALIA.

South Australia.

The map shows that **South Australia** stretches quite across the centre of the continent from north to south. Its name, which was appropriate enough when the colony was first formed, and only included the southern half of its present territory, does not give a true idea of its actual position and boundaries. The great northern section, once called " No Man's Land," was added in 1861.

Most of the population is settled in the south. Should the population of the north ever increase largely, it is probable that the colony would be divided. Since the area is now above 900,000 square miles, or more than France, Germany, Austria, and Italy together, there is enough room for subdivision.

Products of South Australia.

South Australia was first settled in 1836 by free emigrants entirely, and on a plan which was expected to make it chiefly an agricultural country. It has been distinguished among the other colonies for its large production of **wheat**, of which it has long exported a great deal to

Britain, as well as to other parts of Australia. The flour made from its wheat is reckoned among the best in the world.

The climate of the southern or settled parts of the colony is very similar to that of Italy. **Grapes, oranges, lemons, olives,** and similar fruits flourish, and are much cultivated.

Further north and inland the country is too hot and dry for farming, but great flocks of **sheep** are fed on the half-desert pastures, as in other parts of Australia.

Copper mines have been a source of much wealth in South Australia. The **Burra Burra Mines,** discovered in 1845, yielded copper to the value of £700,000 within three years of the time they were opened. Large numbers of English miners went out to work in these mines, and many ships were employed in carrying the ore to England.

The value of the copper obtained from the mines of South Australia up to 1890 was nearly £20,000,000.

Adelaide, the Capital and the largest town, has about 163,000 inhabitants. It is the port at which steamships from England land the mails to be sent on by rail to Melbourne, Sydney, and other parts of Australia. Adelaide is regularly laid out, with wide streets and beautiful public parks and gardens. Behind it is a fine range of mountains, which adds to the beauty of the city.

"Broken Hill."

About 350 miles from Adelaide is the famous silver mine of **Broken Hill,** the richest in the world. It is

approached from South Australia, but is just within the
borders of New South Wales. So late as the year 1880
Broken Hill was only known as a lonely station, in an
almost desert country, where a few sheep were pastured on
the scanty vegetation. But as soon as silver was discovered people crowded to the place, and now it is a town
with about 25,000 inhabitants, and presents a wonderful
scene of busy industry. All along the hill for several
miles are to be seen the huge engines employed in lifting
the ore from the mines, the machinery with which it is
crushed, the furnaces in which it is smelted. Every week
six or seven tons of silver, and many hundreds of tons of
lead with which the silver is mingled, are taken from the
different mines. The railroads are busy carrying the lead
and silver to the sea-coast, where it is shipped to England,
or in bringing back the English goods which fill the shops,
the English coke used in smelting, the English machinery
employed in the works, the food which the people require,
the mining timber which comes from British Columbia or
New Zealand—and many other articles of commerce from
various parts of the world. Thus, in the heart of a desert,
otherwise incapable of supporting any considerable population, a large British community has been built up by the
discovery of a silver mine. So abundant is the ore that
there is no likelihood of its being exhausted for many a
year to come.

South Australian Explorers.

It has been mentioned before that vast deserts cover
much of the central and western portions of Australia.
How terrible these deserts are is best proved by the many

spots in them which mark the graves of adventurous
explorers who, in their efforts to penetrate or cross the
continent, after struggling on for weeks or months, at last
perished for want of food or water. It was not until
1861, and after many attempts had failed, that the
continent was first crossed from south to north.

Ten years later the people of South Australia undertook a splendid, and what was at that time a very difficult,
task. This was to construct a line of telegraph across the
colony from **Adelaide** in the south to **Port Darwin** in the
north. For 1,300 miles of the distance the line had to
be carried through a country only once before traversed,
and then with extreme difficulty, by a small party of
white men. Wells had to be dug along the route to
supply men and animals with water. Provisions, telegraph
posts, the wire itself, and all other appliances, had to be
carried great distances over rocky and sandy deserts. It
took two years of strenuous effort to complete the task.

We may be sure that all this trouble was not taken
merely to reach Port Darwin, then an almost uninhabited
spot. It was for the great purpose of uniting more closely
by means of the telegraph our people in all Australasia
with the people of these British Islands. A cable had
been laid from **Port Darwin** to **Java**, and continued to
India, whence there were already wires to England. Great
numbers of messages are now sent over this long line of
wire every day. Almost every morning we have in English
papers accounts of what was taking place a few hours
before in Australia, and Australian papers have every day
two or three columns of English news of the day before.

K

Business men consult each other and friends talk across all this stretch of ocean and desert. It has been truly said that by telegraphs we have made the whole world one great whispering gallery.

How Melbourne Talks to London.

In passing from Melbourne to London a telegram goes over 13,695 miles of wire, of which 4,408 miles are land lines and 9,287 miles consist of submarine cables. The message cannot be sent the whole of this immense distance at once, but must be repeated at many points.

Here is a list which shows the different points at which it is repeated, and the distance from one point to another.

	Miles.
Melbourne—Mount Gambier	300
Mount Gambier—Adelaide .	270
Adelaide—Port Augusta .	290
Port Augusta—Alice Springs	. 1,036
Alice Springs—Port Darwin	898
Port Darwin—Banjoewangie	. 1,150
Banjoewangie—Batavia	480
Batavia—Singapore .	553
Singapore—Penang	. 399
Penang—Madras .	. 1,280
Madras—Bombay	. 650
Bombay—Aden .	. 1,662
Aden—Suez . .	. 1,346
Suez—Alexandria	. 224
Alexandria—Malta	. 828
Malta—Gibraltar .	. 1,008
Gibraltar—Falmouth	. 1,061
Falmouth—London	. 350

CHAPTER XII.

Western Australia.

Western Australia has a territory extending over more than a million square miles, and is therefore the largest of the Australian colonies.

The country, much of which has not yet been explored, presents a wide field to the adventurous settler. The forests are very extensive and contain many kinds of excellent timber. There is a large export of sandal-wood. On the south and west there are good agricultural lands, and both soil and climate are adapted not only to the growth of wheat, but also of the vine, olive, and fig.

In the inland regions there are known to be vast deserts, some of bare sand, some covered with dense scrub, and others almost impossible to cross from being overgrown with a prickly plant called Spinifex. But before these deserts are reached there is the same pastoral country which extends over so much of the other colonies, and doubtless Western Australia will in time like them become a great sheep- and cattle-raising country.

Within the last few years great deposits of **gold** have been found in and near Coolgardie and Kalgoorlie. A supply of water has been brought by pipes from a distance of more than 300 miles. The yearly output of gold is now about £9,000,000. **Copper** and **lead** are also found, and there is a valuable fishery for **pearls** and **pearl-shell.**

The first settlement was made in 1829. At the request of the colonists themselves, who were much in need of labour, the **Swan River Settlement** was made a convict establishment from 1850 to 1868. Transportation was then finally abolished. Till quite lately Western Australia was a Crown colony. In 1890 it was given a Legislature of its own, and under the new system it is hoped that the colony will develop rapidly.

The capital is **Perth.** Next in importance are **Fremantle** and **Albany.** The latter is situated on **King George's Sound,** an important naval station which is now being strongly fortified at the joint expense of Great Britain and the Australian colonies.

Mail steamships on their way from England to Melbourne and Sydney stop at Fremantle. From Fremantle a line of telegraph has been constructed across the south of the continent to Adelaide, and when the steamships arrive each week a great deal of English news is telegraphed forward to Melbourne, Sydney, and other Australian cities, which it thus reaches some days before the vessels which brought it from England.

Queensland.

Queensland has the large area of about 670,000 square miles, or five and a half times that of the United Kingdom. It occupies the north-eastern portion of the Australian continent, and stretches far up into the Torrid Zone. It has formed a separate colony since 1859, having previously been a part of New South Wales. The vast extent of Queensland, and the difficulty of carrying on the

government of the northern districts from the present
capital, Brisbane, which is on the southern border, makes
it probable that the colony will soon be subdivided.

Products of Queensland.

Lying partly in the Temperate and partly in the Torrid
Zone, Queensland has the productions of both. On the
Darling Downs and other high ground of the southern
districts **wheat, barley, oats,** and other European grains
flourish. Maize is very largely cultivated, and extensive
districts are suited for the growth of **cotton, coffee, tobacco,
oranges,** and **grapes.**

Further north the fertile lands along the coast are
admirably adapted for the culture of the **banana,** the **pine-
apple,** and the **sugar-cane.** As in the other Australian
colonies, **sheep** are largely reared, and on the vast plains
which stretch to the western boundary, **millions of cattle**
are pastured, forming one of the most important features
of pastoral life in Queensland.

The mineral wealth of the colony is also great. Gold
is obtained in many districts, and one mine, **Mount
Morgan,** is perhaps the most valuable and wonderful
deposit of that metal now known in the world.

Mount Morgan.

Mount Morgan is very different from the other mines
in Australia hitherto mentioned, but, in its way, is quite
as wonderful as any of them. It is a low mountain or hill
in the midst of a pastoral country, and apparently not
different from the other hills around it. But all through

the earth and rocks which compose it gold exists so finely distributed that it can seldom be seen with the naked eye. The rocks and earth are ground up into the finest powder, which is then put through a number of chemical processes until the gold is finally extracted from it. This mine has sometimes given to its few fortunate proprietors more than a million pounds sterling a year beyond the cost of working it. Gold-mining here is something very different from that mentioned in connection with the early days of Victoria. There the miners dug up great nuggets, or washed small lumps of gold from the sand. At Mount Morgan the work is less exciting, and usually only the chemists who carry out the final processes of extraction see the gold at all. Cast into bars or ingots, much of it is sent to England direct. Another portion goes to the mints of Sydney or Melbourne, and, if it comes to us, does so in the shape of sovereigns.

Copper, silver, tin, antimony, coal, and other minerals are also found. On the coast the fisheries for pearl and tortoiseshell form an industry of some importance, and bêche-de-mer, a kind of edible sea-slug, is collected in great quantities and exported to China, where it is esteemed a delicacy.

Sugar.

Sugar is one of the important products of Queensland, and sugar plantations are found at intervals along more than 1,200 miles of the coast. In the southern districts much of the work is done by white settlers. Each farmer has a small plantation of his own, and sends his cane,

when ripe, to a mill which manufactures sugar for a
whole district, just as English farmers send their wheat
to the miller to be ground.

Further north the climate of the low-lying sugar
districts on the coast becomes very trying for white men
to work in, and here the cultivation of the plantations
has been chiefly carried on by means of coloured labourers
brought from the Pacific Islands. These **Kanakas,**
as they are called, are hired, like coolies, for a certain
number of years, and then sent back to their homes.

The sugar estates are usually large, and as they are
furnished with expensive machinery and often give employment to hundreds of Kanakas, they require much capital
to carry them on. The direction of the coloured labourers
and the management of those operations in sugar manufacture which require special skill and knowledge furnish
to the English settlers occupations in which they are less
exposed to the heat.

Cattle Runs.

More than six million cattle are fed upon the pasture-
lands of Queensland, and in this particular it surpasses all
the other Australian colonies.

The cattle are reared upon "runs" even larger than
those used for sheep, and sometimes covering many
hundreds of square miles. Here they are cared for by
"stock-riders," or mounted men who spend the whole
day in the saddle in managing and looking after the
herds. From time to time the cattle are "rounded up"
and brought into the stock-yards which are attached to
every cattle station.

The cattle, when fattened, are driven in "mobs" from the remote stations, often over more than a thousand miles, to the markets of Sydney, Melbourne, or Adelaide. All over the pastoral districts of Australia roads are left through the country wide enough for mobs of cattle or sheep to find food upon these long journeys, which often occupy several months.

Besides the cattle sent to these distant markets, other herds are sent to the Queensland coast, where the meat is frozen in the same manner as New Zealand mutton, or preserved in tins, and, with the hides and tallow, shipped to England.

From what has been said we may judge that Queensland has wonderful resources and presents many opportunities for industry and the acquisition of wealth.

To many people the heat of the climate seems a serious drawback, and there are districts in the extreme north where it is not likely that white people will be able to work vigorously and maintain their health. The summer heat of the inland plains, however, is said to be much more easily endured, owing to the dryness of the atmosphere, and the climate of the south and of the more hilly regions is delightful during the greater part of the year.

British emigrants are constantly arriving in the country, and the population is now increasing more rapidly than that of any other Australian colony.

The Barrier Reef.

For more than 1,200 miles along the coast of Queensland stretches the great **Barrier Reef**, a ridge of coral usually nearly level with the sea, but sometimes forming islands.

Its distance from the shore varies from ten to fifty miles. On this reef the waves of the Pacific break and spend their force, leaving the waters within calm for navigation.

The steamships which bring to England the wool, beef, hides, gold, and other products of Queensland sail northward between this Barrier Reef and the mainland, and then find their way out into the Indian Ocean through the **Torres Straits.**

Thursday Island, at the northern extremity of Queensland, commands the entrance to the Torres Straits, and for that reason is being strongly fortified as a coaling and naval station. It is also the chief port for vessels engaged in the pearl-fisheries of the neighbouring seas. as well as the centre of the trade carried on with New Guinea.

Water Supply and Irrigation in Australia.

Many parts of Australia are subject to prolonged droughts. These droughts are often followed by heavy rains, which fill up the shallow water-courses, and even cause extensive floods. When the rains have ceased the water soon sinks again into the sandy soil.

These circumstances have made people try many plans to save a sufficient supply of water to carry them through the dry season.

Sometimes the farmer or squatter simply excavates, in

some hollow where he finds a clay bottom, a reservoir large enough to hold water sufficient for his wants from one rainy season to another. Or the people of a whole district unite together, and at great expense construct a much larger reservoir, holding millions of gallons of water, from which all receive what they require to water their flocks or irrigate their fields.

In many places, where neither of these plans can be carried out, it is found possible to get a constant supply from a great depth beneath the soil by boring what are called Artesian wells.

In a few localities where considerable streams flow through desert-land experiments of another kind are being tried on a large scale. By means of powerful machinery water is pumped up from the streams in sufficient quantity to irrigate thousands of acres of the dry soil, which, when thus watered, is found to be exceedingly fertile. So where before there was nothing to be seen but sand and desert scrub, there soon grow up whole villages, surrounded by orange-groves, vineyards, and fertile fields.

It is wonderful how much has been done by means like these to lessen the dangers of drought, and to make districts once considered deserts, habitable and capable of supporting flocks and herds.

Homeward Route from Australia.

And now it is time to leave Australia. From Australia there is a choice of several routes by which to return to England. The one now most commonly used by travellers, because the shortest, is that through the Indian Ocean, the

Red Sea, the Suez Canal, and the Mediterranean. The one chiefly used before the Suez Canal was opened was that round the Cape of Good Hope. A third is round Cape Horn in South America, and a fourth across the Pacific, the North American Continent, and the Atlantic. Some lines of steamships make the outward voyage from England by way of the Cape of Good Hope, and return round Cape Horn, thus completing a voyage round the world at each trip.

Leaving Australia from Adelaide we have a voyage of nearly 6,000 miles to reach the continent of **Africa**. **St. Paul's** and **Kerguelen Islands** lie along this route, but are seldom used as stopping-places save by ships driven to them in stormy weather. They are, however, reckoned among British possessions. **Cape Town** is the port of South Africa at which we arrive.

◆◆◆

CHAPTER XIII.

AFRICA.

We have now come to another great continent. If we examine the map of Africa we find that the position of British people there is very different from what it is on other continents. In North America the only nation near us is the United States, whose people are partly of British descent like ourselves, and speak our language. In Australia and New Zealand we have been left alone to carry on colonisation. Later we shall learn that in Asia other

European nations have retired from India and left its government almost entirely to Great Britain.

In South Africa the case is quite different. In that country several other nations are trying to establish colonies. Our possessions border upon those of the **Germans**, the

FIG. 53.—BRITISH POSSESSIONS IN AFRICA.

French, the **Portuguese**, and the **Italians**; upon the **Congo State**, which is chiefly controlled by **Belgians**, as well as upon the territories of independent native tribes. Several European nations seem, within the last few years, to have suddenly made up their minds to take possession of all they can get of Africa, the only continent still remaining to be occupied by white men. Meanwhile our own

people are pushing rapidly forward to make new settlements in different directions, especially towards the centre
of the great continent.

The Race for Africa.

This mixture of nationalities makes the management of
our affairs in Africa a very difficult business. We have to

FIG. 34.—SOUTH AFRICA.

guard the rights of our own settlers who are colonising
parts of the country, and at the same time to consider what
is just to other nations who are doing the same, and what
is just to the native races.

Great trouble has therefore been taken to make agree-
ments with other European nations, settling in a peaceful
way the limits within which each will be free to trade or
colonise. Treaties have thus been made with Germany,
France, Portugal, and Italy.

On the other hand, further treaties must be made with
the many native tribes, so that they may willingly
allow our traders and colonists to come into the country.
So we may be sure that all the prudence of a great many
wise heads is required to manage our affairs in Africa.

Climate and Colonisation in Africa.

As European people have only lately begun to explore
and settle many parts of the African continent, and as
great changes are constantly going on, it is impossible in
all cases to mark the boundaries of our territories as pre-
cisely as on the other continents.   One fact, however, we
should notice particularly, for it has a great deal to do
with the future growth of the Empire in Africa.   A large
part of the country which we have formed into colonies, or
which we are only beginning to occupy, is either in the
southern part of the continent or on highlands in the
interior.   In both cases we have the great advantage of a
cool climate which is favourable for people of a northern
race.   It therefore seems probable that the regions under
British control will become the homes of white people
much more than the territories held by other nations.

Cape Colony.

Of the portions of the Empire in Africa, **Cape Colony**
is at present the most important.   Like Canada, it was not
at first settled by British people.   It was in 1497, five
years after Columbus discovered America, that **Vasco da
Gama**, a Portuguese navigator, first found the way to India
around the Cape of Good Hope.   In later years, Por-

tuguese, Dutch, and English ships often stopped at the Cape
on their way to the East, but no fixed settlement was made
for more than 150 years. In 1652 the **Dutch** first formed
a colony at Table Bay, which remained under the rule of
Holland for nearly a century and a half. All the settlers

FIG. 35.—CAPE TOWN AND TABLE MOUNTAIN.

were Dutch, except some hundreds of **French Protestants,**
who found homes here in 1688 after being expelled from
their own country, and whose descendants soon adopted
the Dutch language instead of their own.

In 1795 England, which was then at war with France
and Holland, took forcible possession of the colony, but
restored it to Holland at the Peace of 1803. Only three

years later, in 1806, war having again broken out, an
English force once more captured the Cape. At the peace
which followed, in 1814, England agreed to pay between
two and three millions sterling to the King of the Nether-
lands on condition that the colony should be finally ceded
to her. Our first possessions in South Africa, then, were
secured partly by conquest and partly by purchase.

Dutchmen, Englishmen, and Natives.

We can now understand why it is that a large
number of our fellow-subjects at the Cape of Good Hope
are of Dutch descent and speak the Dutch language.
Dutch and English may both be used in the Cape Parliament, just as French and English may both be used in
the Canadian Parliament. The **Dutch Boer**, as the de-
scendant of the old colonists is called, clings to his language and customs as closely as the French *habitant* of
Quebec does to his. But Dutch and English do not
make up the whole, or even the chief part, of the population of the Cape Colony. In this the Cape differs from
our other great colonies.

In Canada the Red Indian, in New Zealand the
Maori, in Australia and Tasmania the dark-skinned
natives, are all gradually disappearing as white men
settle in the country. This is not the case with the
Hottentots, Kaffirs, and other native races of Africa, who
increase rather than diminish under English rule. It is
quite clear that in our African colonies we shall always
have a large coloured population. In Cape Colony the
natives at present far outnumber those of European

descent. Of a total population of about 2,400,000 less than 500,000 are whites.

Until a few years ago the Dutch and English settlers at the Cape were engaged in frequent wars with the different native races. The latter now live peacefully under British rule, and large numbers have even removed into British territory to enjoy the protection from their enemies which our flag gives them.

Climate and Products of South Africa.

In climate, soil, and productions, South Africa has many points of resemblance to Australia. It has the same warm, dry climate, and wide stretches of partly desert country, subject to droughts, but supporting large flocks and herds, and, in rainy seasons, or when irrigated, very fertile. It produces **wool** and **gold**, and is a **grape-growing** country.

But, unlike Australia, South Africa is a mountainous country. One great mountain range stretches for more than 1,000 miles parallel to the coast, never more than 100 or 150 miles distant from it. Behind this are other ranges, the plains between them forming a series of terraces.

The Great Karroo.

Between the two upper ranges is an elevated tract known as the Great "Karroo"—the word itself meaning a dry or barren district. The Great Karroo stretches 300 miles from west to east, and has a breadth of 70 miles. The Karroo country embraces in all about 48,000,000 acres, and on it are pastured five or six millions of sheep.

L

A strange region it is, as may be gathered from the following description :—

"This large, marvellous tract of country, which has been regarded as semi-desert, is as fertile as the banks of the Nile, provided it receives sufficient moisture. But even the severest drought cannot destroy its vegetation. You look around for miles and miles and see nothing but dusty ground and small stumps of bushes sparingly strewn over the surface; not a green leaf, not a blade of grass, except, at long intervals, rows of mimosa trees along the dry beds of rivers. You think this is desolation, a life-destroying desert. But at last you notice a building at the distance; you see trees near the house; you get to a farm, you are hospitably received, are treated with coffee and bokhe mélk (goat's milk) ; the old man shows you his fountain (spring) which he has newly opened up by aid of dynamite; he shows you his steam-engine to pump up water for the flocks, his dam that cost him hundreds of pounds, his garden with wonderful wheat and oats, splendid fruit-trees, enormous pumpkins. He tells you, Yes, it is ' banj droog ' (very dry) ; during three years there has been rain only twice or three times ; his lambs are lost, he had to cut their throats to save the ewes, and many of his big sheep are dead also, but the remainder are all right; as long as his fountain runs he has no fear; while they have water, they keep alive on the stumps of the bushes. And when rain, good rain comes, then all these bushes revive ; there is a general resurrection, grass springs up, and there is an abundance of food for the flocks, which, after first suffering from the sudden change, soon prosper and increase as nowhere else in the world."

In these Karroo regions the farmers have another occupation besides sheep-raising, and one which is peculiar to the country.

Ostrich Farming.

Ostrich farming has become of much importance in South Africa during the last few years. It is a singular industry, and interesting, because it furnishes a striking example of how a new and profitable employment may be created by men who give patient thought and attention to a subject.

We have all seen ostrich feathers, and perhaps know that for ages they have been prized as ornaments, and looked upon as among the most beautiful productions of nature. We have probably read in history how, as far back as the year 1346, our English Black Prince, at the battle of Crecy, took the plume of ostrich feathers from the helmet of the slain King of Bohemia, and that ever since an ostrich plume has formed the crest of our Princes of Wales. .

During all these centuries, till a few years ago, the only way of getting these beautiful feathers was by hunting and killing the birds in Africa, where alone they were found. So eagerly were they pursued by black hunters and white that they seemed likely soon to be entirely destroyed.

But about the year 1865 attempts began to be made by farmers at Cape Colony to tame the ostrich, hitherto one of the wildest and least approachable of birds.

The plan of artificially hatching the eggs in *incubators* was widely adopted, and by close study of the peculiar habits of the birds it was found possible to rear the young ones and gradually domesticate them. Much difficulty and many failures were met with at first, but within twenty years ostrich farming had become such a settled industry that the number of domesticated birds in the colony was estimated at 150,000, and the export of feathers in a single year had risen to above £1,000,000. Thanks to the persevering skill of the Cape farmers, there is now no fear that the race of ostriches will become extinct, or the supply of feathers run short.

In the next chapter we shall find an account of a visit to a large ostrich farm.

CHAPTER XIV.

AN AFRICAN INDUSTRY.

A Visit to an Ostrich Farm.

"The size of the farm is 13,000 acres, situated in the Eastern Province of the Cape Colony. The herbage is a mixture of grass, karoo (a sort of heather), and succulent bushes. The rainfall in this part of the Eastern Province is too uncertain to allow of cultivation without irrigation, so the cultivation is confined to a few acres of lucerne irrigated by pumps, some soft green food being indispensable for rearing the little ostrich chicks during droughts. On the farm are kept 600 ostriches and 400 breeding cattle. The whole property is enclosed by strong wire fences

five feet high, and subdivided into numerous camps with
similar fences. Near the homestead the camps are of about
100 acres each, being appropriated to the rearing of the
young birds. Beyond these again are camps of about
25 acres each, these being given up to a single pair of
superior old birds in each camp for breeding; whilst beyond
these again are large camps of about 2,600 acres in extent,
with 150 birds in each.

" But let us take a stroll in these camps, and see what
is going on. Here in the first we find an old Hottentot,
with about thirty little ostriches only a few days old around
him. These have all been hatched in the incubator, and
he is doing nurse to them, cutting up lucerne for them
to eat, supplying them with fine gravel to fill their gizzards
with to grind their food, breaking up bones that they may
get a supply of phosphates, and giving them wheat and
water; and at sundown he will bring them back to the
incubator for warmth, or, should the weather change and
rain come on, he will be seen hurrying home with his
thirty little children following him to a warm, well-lighted
room, with a clean-sanded floor.

" In the next camp we have a pair of birds and about
fifteen chicks, accompanied by a Kaffir man, who has been
with them every day from the time they were hatched, to
get them tamed and accustomed to man. These have been
hatched by the parent birds, who will brood them at night
in the camp. But great risks are run by this method of
rearing, from wild carnivorous animals catching the chicks,
as great numbers of carnivorous animals of nearly every
known species abound in South Africa; the most destruc-

tive to young ostriches being the jackals, a single one of which will destroy a whole brood in a night. Our host informs us that he is compelled to keep a man constantly employed laying poison and setting traps.

" But here we come to another camp, in which we are told there is a nest, and as we enter, a heavy thorn-bush is given to us, and we are told that if the male bird charges we are to hold it to his eyes. But we do not see the cock bird, and have got some distance in, and can just see the hen bird upon the nest, with its neck stretched along the ground, making itself look as much as possible like one of the monster ant-heaps that abound in the country, when we are startled by three tremendous roars behind us, and only just have time to put up our bush when the infuriated cock charges down as fast as a horse can gallop, making every nerve in our body shiver with fear, as we remember having heard of broken ribs and legs, and men killed by savage male birds; but we follow the example of our conductor, and keep the bush at a level with the bird's eyes, when just as he reaches the bush he stops suddenly, his instinct teaching him not to risk his eyesight against the thorns. Then we move on to the nest, keeping the cock at bay with our bushes; but we are thankful when it is over, as the cock dodges round us, first on this side, then on that, always trying to get his head past our bush; and, should he succeed, he would instantly floor us with a kick from his foot, armed as it is with the formidable horny nail. The kick is delivered forward and downwards, and with immense force when at the height of a man's breast, gradually losing its force as the foot nears the ground, in consequence of which many men have saved their lives, when attacked unprepared, by lying flat on the ground, thereby escaping with a severe trampling, but no broken bones.

"We, however, arrive at the nest without accident, when to our astonishment our conductor suddenly lays his bush down, and handles the eggs, and we find that the hitherto infuriated cock's nature has quite changed; he that a moment ago was trying with all his might to get at us and kill us, now stands a dejected, beseeching creature, uttering a plaintive noise, and beseeching us in every possible way not to break his eggs. The nest we find to be merely a scratched hollow in a sandy place, with fifteen eggs in it, weighing three pounds each, upon which the parent birds must sit for six weeks, the cock sitting by night and the hen by day, the eggs being exposed to many risks of destruction by jackals, baboons, and carrion crows, or by heavy rains filling the nest with water. The *modus operandi* of the carrion crows to get at the contents of the eggs is very ingenious; their bills are not strong enough to break the shell, so they take a good-sized stone in their claws, and, rising up to a considerable height, let it drop on the eggs, but, unless there are suitable stones near the nest, they cannot do this, seeming not to be able to carry the stones horizontally.

"But now we arrive at one of the large camps with a troop of 150 well-grown birds in it, and here in the corner we have a planked yard; this is where the birds are plucked, the one end being movable, so that when the birds are in, the end can be moved up and the birds packed in so closely that they have no room to kick. Just as we enter we observe the birds coming over the hill, being driven by ten men on horseback, each man carrying his thorn-bush to turn a refractory bird or to master a savage cock. The birds being yarded, the plucking begins; the tails and long

FIG. 36.—OSTRICHES.

black and drab feathers are pulled out, the white feathers being cut off, and the stumps left for two months, till the quill is ripe, this being done to get the feather before it is damaged, and the quill being left in so as not to injure the socket by pulling it before it is ready to be shed.

"We now return to the homestead, and visit the incubator-room, which is constructed to be as little affected by changes of temperature as possible. Then we visit the feather-room, and see the feathers being sorted into the different qualities, and done up in bunches, either for sale in the colony or for shipment to England. We then visit the kraals, and find some seventy or eighty cows being milked, as dairy farming can be most successfully carried on in conjunction with ostrich farming; the cattle eating the coarser grasses, and tending to keep the bush from getting too thick for the ostriches to pass amongst it. We find all the labour on the farm is done by natives, who make excellent servants for managing stock; and as the natives are exceedingly fond of milk, the ostrich farmer, who has an unlimited amount of milk to give them, greatly reduces the cost of their food, and makes them contented and happy."

Such are some of the sights that may be seen on an ostrich farm.

CHAPTER XV.

BRITISH POSSESSIONS IN AFRICA.

Mohair.

Another way in which South African farmers have added to the wealth and resources of their country deserves to be mentioned.

Mohair is much used in English factories for making some kinds of cloth. It is obtained from the **Angora goat,** which is a native of Asia. Formerly English supplies of mohair came chiefly from Asia Minor, Turkey in Europe, and other countries around the Mediterranean. Between

1850 and 1860 the Angora goat was introduced into Cape Colony, as it was believed that the climate and soil would be suited for rearing it successfully. In 1862 only 1,036 lbs. of mohair were sold, but thirteen years later the sale had increased to more than 5,000,000 lbs., and it is now one of the considerable exports of the country. Just as Australia and New Zealand, by the introduction of sheep, have become the greatest wool-growing countries in the world, so it seems as if South Africa may be made the greatest mohair-producing country.

Diamonds.

South Africa possesses the richest **diamond mines** in the world. For ages diamonds have been the most highly prized of all precious stones. Their extreme hardness makes them of great use for a few mechanical purposes, such as cutting glass, and making drills to penetrate the hardest rocks. But their value has always depended on their beauty as an ornament more than upon their utility.

Rich people have always been ready to pay large sums for a jewel which was at once rare and beautiful.

In ancient times diamonds were chiefly obtained in India, and formed part of the trade with that country. Then, after the discovery of America, the mines of Brazil became very famous. But the mines of South Africa, first discovered about twenty-five years ago, have far surpassed in value and productiveness all that were known before. Great fortunes have been made in working them, and more than £1,000,000 worth has sometimes been exported in a single year.

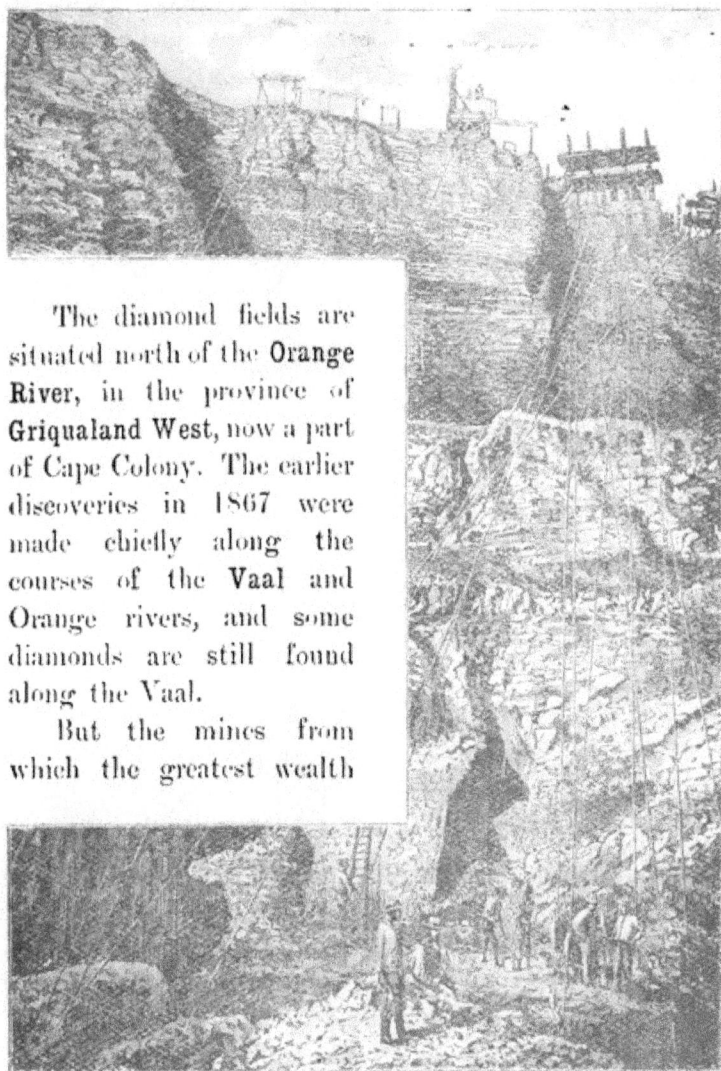

The diamond fields are situated north of the **Orange River**, in the province of **Griqualand West**, now a part of Cape Colony. The earlier discoveries in 1867 were made chiefly along the courses of the **Vaal** and Orange rivers, and some diamonds are still found along the Vaal.

But the mines from which the greatest wealth

FIG. 37.   MINES AT KIMBERLEY

has been derived were discovered in 1871 where the town of **Kimberley** now stands. That town has now a large population, depending almost entirely upon the operations going on in the four chief mines, **Bulfontein**, **De Beer**, **Du Toit's Pan**, and **Kimberley**, all of which are mining stations situated within two or three miles of each other.

From this small district more than £40,000,000 worth of diamonds have been taken since the mines were opened.

Natal.

Natal, situated on the south-east coast of Africa, has an area of about 24,000 square miles, and a population numbering approximately 925,000—of whom not a twelfth are white.

The first European settlement was made in 1824 by Englishmen, who were a few years later followed by Dutch Boers migrating from Cape Colony.

The new settlement was at first annexed to the Cape, but it was in 1856 made an independent colony.

The country is naturally divided into three districts or belts, differing in character and productions.

The coast region extends inland about fifteen or sixteen miles. It has a tropical climate and a very fertile soil, which produces **sugar, tea, coffee, indigo, rice, tobacco, cotton,** and **pine-apples.**

Behind the coast region is a higher hilly country with green pastures, and here **wheat, oats,** and **barley,** the **potato,** and other English crops flourish.

Further inland, the land rises to mountain ranges and

large upland plains, chiefly suited for rearing **sheep** and **cattle**.

The population is curiously mixed. Among the whites, the English outnumber the Dutch; Natal differing from Cape Colony, where the Dutch are most numerous. The Natives are of many tribes, and consist mostly of those who have, in consequence of wars, fled into the colony to be safe under the British flag. As they are either lazy or prefer cultivating their own fields, Hindoo coolies, to the number of nearly 40,000, have been introduced to do the work of the plantations.

Other British Possessions Crown Colonies.

Besides the colonies already mentioned, we have in South Africa taken under our control or protection several regions which are inhabited almost entirely by the native races.

BECHUANALAND lies to the north of Cape Colony. It consists of two parts: one, comprising about 50,000 square miles, which has now been added to the Cape Colony, another covering 162,000 square miles, which was formerly a "Protectorate" * under the British Government, but which is now partly governed by the "British South Africa Company," of which we shall read further on. Much of Bechuanaland is poorly watered, but the climate is good, and the region seems likely to grow into an important colony.

---

* The term *Protectorate* is used to denote a region over which our Government, without assuming complete possession, claims the right to exercise a limited control, to the exclusion of other European nations.

BASUTOLAND is a small Crown colony, between Cape Colony and Natal. It extends over about 10,000 square miles, and has a population of nearly 265,000, only a few hundreds being Europeans. It is well watered, with fine pastures, on which the natives rear great herds of cattle.

FIG. 38.—ZULUS.

It is said to have the best grain-producing soil of any district in South Africa.

ZULULAND is a country inhabited by a warlike people, with whom a few years ago we had a serious war. Finding that it was impossible to establish a firm native Government, it was decided in 1887 to make Zululand a British colony; but native disputes are settled by native law, and Europeans are not allowed to settle on the land, except for trading, mining, and missionary purposes.

The Governor of Natal also acts as Governor of Zululand.

The Transvaal and Orange River Colony.

The **TRANSVAAL** and the **ORANGE FREE STATE**

FIG. 20. "TREKKING."

were settled by Dutch colonists from the Cape who were dissatisfied with English government, and so removed (or, to use the South African expression, *trekked*) further into the interior of the country, and formed new settlements. In 1854 both the Transvaal and the Orange Free State were recognised as independent States by the English Government.

The Transvaal was annexed to the Empire in 1877. To this annexation the Boers offered a vigorous resistance, and the English troops sent to put down opposition were defeated. A treaty was then made by which the continued independence of the country was agreed to.

Many British colonists settled in the Republics, but they were not granted the same privileges of citizenship as the Boers, and in addition were heavily taxed. The British Government tried to get these grievances remedied, but unsuccessfully, and at the end of 1899 the two Republics declared war. After much fighting, in which Volunteers from all parts of the Empire came forward in thousands to fight side by side with the English troops, the Boers were defeated and their land was once more, in 1902, annexed to the British Empire. The territories are now known as **THE TRANSVAAL COLONY** and **THE ORANGE RIVER COLONY.**

Trading Companies in Africa.

We have already pointed out that in many cases colonies were founded for trading purposes. Indeed, it may truly be said that it is chiefly as a race of traders that we have spread our influence over so large a portion of the world. When we come to study about India, we shall find that nearly all our vast possessions there were gained for us, and were for a long time governed, by a company of English merchants. We have also found that for many years more than half of Canada was held and controlled by another such company.

In Africa some remarkable attempts have been made

of late years to open up extensive regions to commerce in the same way. Large portions of the continent have been placed under the control of what are known as "Chartered Companies." These companies are formed and carry on their work in the following way :—

A number of merchants or wealthy men join together, and subscribe a large sum of money to carry out the purposes they have in view. They then lay their plans before the Imperial Government and obtain from it a "**Royal Charter**," which entitles them to trade over a certain area of country, to make treaties with the native tribes, to establish a force of police for maintaining peace and order, and to frame and carry out laws for the good government of their territory. Agents, officers, and men are then sent out ; stores and forts are erected at convenient points ; steamship communication is established ; roads are made ; railway and telegraph lines are constructed ; and the work of opening up trade and civilising the country is carried forward actively. Usually such a company agrees to do all it can to put down slavery, which is the great curse of the African continent.

There have been two great British companies of this kind governing or exercising their influence over regions in Africa, each as large as European States.

The **ROYAL NIGER COMPANY** at one time had control over more than 100,000 square miles of country in the valley of the **Niger**, and along the coast near the mouth of that river. The company maintained a large fleet of river steamers, and had a force of about 500 coloured soldiers, under European officers, together with police in each

M

district.   A large trade was done with the natives in exchanging English manufactured goods for ivory, rubber,
palm-oil, gum-arabic, copal, hides, and other products.

British East Africa.

There is one more large piece of African territory
which must be mentioned here because, though it is now
under the British Government, it was formerly, like the
district of which we have just read, under the control of a
Chartered Company known as the **IMPERIAL BRITISH
EAST AFRICA COMPANY.** This Company had for several
years under its management a large territory on the eastern
side of Africa, the coast line of which extended from the
Umba River in the south to the **Juba** in the north: a
distance of 400 miles.   It stretched inland to the borders
of the **Congo State**, and to the waters of the **Nile.** The
Company did not succeed very well, and at last it was
decided that the time had come to put an end to it.

Under the rule of the Company a railway was projected
from **Mombasa**, the principal harbour, to **Lake Victoria
Nyanza**; trade roads were opened to the interior; steamships
placed upon the rivers and Lake Victoria Nyanza; and
different points were connected by telegraph. The exports of this region are various, and include **ivory, hides,
indiarubber, cloves, gums, ebony, rhinoceros horn** and
hippopotamus teeth, tobacco, cattle, sheep, and **goats.**

In past times, and until very lately, the greatest export
of all was that of **slaves,** and to put down this trade was
one of the main objects of the Government.   It is believed
that nothing will help more towards putting an end to it

than the making of roads and railways. The Arab traders formerly brought down ivory on the backs of slaves. Railways and roads will not only make this unprofitable, but will enable us easily to reach the heart of the country to check Arab cruelties.

The British Government has now assumed full control of this large section of Africa.

The **BRITISH SOUTH AFRICA COMPANY** has undertaken to open up a vast territory, called **Zambesia**, in the heart of Africa, south of the **River Zambesi**. **MASHONA-LAND**, a portion of this region, is rich in gold, and is also a good pastoral and agricultural country, suitable for European settlement. A railway is being built and a telegraph line has been extended northwards from Cape Colony, through Bechuanaland towards Cairo. The country is also reached from the eastern coast.

Portuguese Territory.

We may see on the map that in order to get by the shortest way from the coast to Zambesia, it is necessary to pass through the strip of Portuguese territory which stretches along the east of Africa, from **Delagoa Bay** to **Cape Delegado**. This circumstance has caused trouble with the Portuguese, and furnishes an example of those difficulties which we meet with from having to deal with the various nations who occupy parts of Africa.

The Duty of the British Government.

These trading companies are not left entirely to themselves in the government of the regions in which their operations are carried on. It is the duty of one of the Queen's ministers, the Secretary of State for Foreign Affairs, to see that nothing is done in their dealing with the native races of which the people of England do not approve. This is very necessary; for often in our history it has been found that the eagerness of traders and colonists to get all the advantage possible out of a new country has led them to act unjustly towards the weaker races with whom they have to deal.

We now see that the influence of Britain as a trading, colonising, and civilising country is from several directions being rapidly pushed into the heart of the " Dark Continent," as Africa has long been called. We may be sure that if we act wisely and justly, great good will be done for the native races. As peace and good government are established it is found that the people settle down to steady industry, and are able to produce articles of commerce, in exchange for which they may secure many things that add to their comfort and happiness. Besides this, the horrible slave-trade is gradually put down, and teachers and missionaries have an opportunity to instruct the natives, and so lift them out of their state of ignorance and barbarism.

West Africa.

There are some things in the earlier relations of our country with the West Coast of Africa which are not pleasant to remember.

Before slavery was abolished in the British dominions, and when negroes were wanted to work on the plantations of the West Indies and North America, it was on this coast that the barbarous slave-trade was chiefly carried on. The vessels of the slave-traders infested the coast, captured the unfortunate negroes, or purchased the captives taken in war from the native chiefs, who were thus encouraged to keep up the most cruel and constant strife with each other.

After the trade was made illegal in 1807, and slavery itself was abolished in 1833, our colonies on the West Coast of Africa became of importance in connection with our efforts to put an end to the inhuman traffic.

Sierra Leone.

In 1787 an English company was formed to establish a colony in Africa for the reception of freed negroes, of whom there were then a good many in England. These were collected and sent out to what is now called **Freetown**, the capital of the colony, where a grant of land had been obtained from a native chief. These first colonists were joined at a later period by other freed negroes from Nova Scotia and Jamaica, and after 1807, when the Government took charge of the colony, whole cargoes of negroes, saved from slave-trading ships, and who could not be returned to their own homes, were landed and settled here. Thus the population is composed of the descendants of many African tribes.

Of late years **Sierra Leone** has been considered very important as a coaling station, and for the protection of our trade to the Cape of Good Hope and the East. Batteries armed with heavy guns have been erected for the protection of its excellent harbour. The climate is

not a good one for white men, and this causes a difficulty
in providing the fortifications with a sufficient garrison.

Hitherto the troops kept there have belonged to the
West India Regiments, which are composed of negroes,
but the number of English troops on the station will
probably be largely increased.

The population of Sierra Leone and the adjoining

FIG. 40.—CAPE COAST CASTLE, ON THE GOLD COAST.

islands is over 76,000, but the resident white population
does not now number much more than 400.

GAMBIA lies to the north from Sierra Leone.   It has
an area of 69 square miles, with a population of about
14,000 persons, of whom very few are white.   At one
time Gambia was a great centre of the slave-trade.

The GOLD COAST, stretching along the northern
shore of the Gulf of Guinea for about 350 miles, has an area

of about 39,000 square miles, and a population estimated at nearly a million and a half souls. **Gold** is found in considerable quantities. It was obtained by the Portuguese and French in the fourteenth, fifteenth, and sixteenth centuries, and at present about £80,000 worth each year is obtained for export.

LAGOS is a small island lying off what was formerly known as the Slave Coast, and was taken possession of by the British Government in order to suppress the slave-trade, of which it was the head-quarters for this part of Africa. Other islands and a portion of the neighbouring mainland have been added to the colony, which has a population numbering 1,500,000. Lagos has the only safe harbour found along 600 miles of coast, and has therefore become the chief seat of commerce for the neighbouring territories. The city is the wealthiest and most populous on the West Coast of Africa.

St. Helena.

Along the track of ships going from Europe to India by the Cape of Good Hope is the island of **St. Helena**, which has belonged to Britain ever since 1673, when it was captured from the Dutch.

Before the opening of the Suez Canal it was of great importance as a port of call for ships in the Indian trade, which stopped here for water and fresh provisions. It is now so little used that the population of the island has greatly decreased, and the force of soldiers once maintained for its defence has been much reduced. It has, however, strong fortifications. Should the Suez Canal

FIG. 41.—ST. HELENA.

ever be closed to our trade, St. Helena would at once become as important as in former times.

The island is 10½ miles long and 6½ miles broad, and is about a third of the size of the Isle of Wight. Lofty cliffs, from 600 to 2,400 feet in height, face the sea on all sides, giving the island a desolate and forbidding aspect. The soil is in many parts fertile, and furnishes excellent pasturage, while the island is well watered. The whole population numbers about 5,000.

St. Helena has been made famous in history from having been the place where Napoleon Bonaparte was kept in exile after his final defeat by Wellington at Waterloo.

Thousands of Boer prisoners were confined in St. Helena during the Boer War of 1901–2.

Ascension.

Eight hundred miles northward from St. Helena is the equally lonely island of **Ascension.** We took possession of it in 1815, probably as a part of our precautions in watching over Bonaparte at St. Helena. The station of **Georgetown,** situated on a small bay on the western coast, is protected by a fort. The place has an excellent hospital, to which the sick may be sent from ships which touch there.

Ascension has been chiefly used as a victualling place for vessels employed in suppressing the slave-trade on the African coast, and for those engaged in the southern whale fisheries. In time of war it might become of considerable importance as one of the links in our line of communication with the East. It has been described as a fixed store-ship of the navy, and as such is under the control of the Admiralty.

The area of the island is 35 square miles, and the population numbers about 430. **Sea-turtles** constitute almost the only article of commerce. They are caught in large numbers, weighing from 600 to 800 lbs. each.

CHAPTER XVI.

BRITISH STRONGHOLDS IN THE MEDITERRANEAN.

The Mediterranean Sea.

THE great trading and civilising nations of old times, such as the Jews, Phœnicians, Greeks, Romans, and Carthaginians, were settled around the **Mediterranean Sea.** Most

FIG. 12.—THE MEDITERRANEAN.

of the commerce of the ancient world was carried on around its shores. At a later time the Republics of Venice and Genoa rose to great power and influence, chiefly owing to the good position for trading purposes which they occupied on the same sea. The wealth of all these nations came partly from the fact that it was only by way of the

Mediterranean that the rich productions of the far East could reach Europe.

When the new route to India and China by way of the Cape of Good Hope was discovered, in 1497, the commercial importance of the Mediterranean declined, for it was found easier to bring goods from the East by sea than overland across the Isthmus of Suez to the Mediterranean.

But all this was once more changed in 1868, when the **Suez Canal** was opened, and a large part of the vastly increased flood of Eastern commerce began again to come to Europe by way of the Red Sea and the Mediterranean. As most of this trade is British, or carried on under the British flag, the interests which we have to guard in the Mediterranean are very great, even if we only look upon that sea as connecting us with parts of our own Empire.

We have long maintained here places of great strength, which are of much importance for the protection of our commerce.

Gibraltar.

On the northern side of the Straits of Gibraltar is a promontory of rock, joined to the mainland of Spain by a sandy isthmus. At the highest point it rises to about 1,400 feet above the level of the sea. This Rock of **Gibraltar** we captured from the Spaniards in 1704. Many attempts have since been made to re-take it, especially between the years 1779 and 1783, when for three years and seven months our garrison there had to sustain a siege against the combined French and Spanish forces.

Very large sums of British money have been spent in strengthening the fortifications, and we usually keep there

FIG. 43.—GIBRALTAR.

a garrison of about 5,000 men. Batteries have been constructed at many advantageous points, while on the landward side, and also so as to command the bay, two ranges of galleries have been cut out of the solid rock, and furnished with heavy cannon.

Gibraltar is therefore now commonly considered one of the strongest fortresses in the world. Its whole area is only about two square miles, and it is the smallest dependency of the Empire. But it is a

FIG. 44.—STRAIT OF GIBRALTAR.

very important one. Situated at the mouth of the Mediterranean, it serves to protect our trade in that great sea. As a coaling station, it supplies steamships engaged in the Eastern, Australian, and Mediterranean trade, and those which ply along the Western coast of Africa as well.

As the place is chiefly important as a fortress, its governor is always a military officer of high rank. Besides the British garrison, the town has a population of about 13,000 persons, chiefly of Spanish and Maltese descent. When foreigners wish to enter the town or to live there, they can only do so by getting permission from the military authorities.

Malta.

While Gibraltar guards the mouth of the Mediterranean, the position which we hold at **Malta**, in the centre of that great sea, is scarcely less important. Situated between Sicily and Africa, and about half-way between Gibraltar and Port Said, Malta lies in the direct route of the main traffic which passes through the Suez Canal. Upon it we chiefly rely for the defence of our commerce within the Mediterranean. It is the head-quarters of our Mediterranean fleet, and a port of call for most of the great steamship lines to the East.

We obtained possession of Malta in 1800, when, after the expulsion of the French, the islands composing the group were ceded to Great Britain by the inhabitants. The two principal islands are **Malta** and **Gozo**, with several smaller ones, and the total area is about 117 square miles, with a population of nearly 188,000 people, exclusive of the six or eight thousand British soldiers usually kept in garrison there. For 264 years, from 1534 to 1798, Malta was occupied by the **Knights of St. John**, a military brotherhood, organised to defend the Holy Sepulchre at Jerusalem, and to resist the " infidels," or Turks, who then threatened to overrun Europe. These knights spent large sums of money in constructing fortifications, and much more has been done since the British occupation to add to the strength of the fortress. In the magazines, stores of water, material, and provisions are always kept, sufficient

FIG. 15.—HARBOUR OF VALETTA.

Charles W. Wyllie

FIG. 46. GRAND HARBOUR, VALETTA

to enable the place to sustain a prolonged siege.
Valetta, the principal town, has an excellent harbour,
around which are grouped the more important fortifications.

Cyprus.

The island of **Cyprus**, at the eastern extremity of the
Mediterranean, is not a part of the British Empire, nor

FIG. 17.—CYPRUS.

are its people British
subjects, but both are
at present in the keep-
ing of the British
Government, which
administers justice,
collects taxes, and is
responsible for the
welfare of the people.
The control of this
island was obtained
in 1878 from Turkey,
as a position from
which the advance of
Russia in Asia Minor could be watched, and, if necessary, checked. Although we keep a small body of troops
there, we have made no attempt to change it into a
strongly fortified post, as seems at first to have been
intended. The trade of Cyprus has largely increased
under British rule, and the administration of justice has
been much improved. We pay a subsidy of £92,800
each year to the Sultan of Turkey for giving us the
control of Cyprus. This sum is chiefly derived from the

revenues of the island, but a portion is paid by vote of Parliament.

Gibraltar, Malta, and **Cyprus,** then, are the three dependencies which we hold in the Mediterranean, and by which we maintain our national position there.

Note.—From Plymouth to Gibraltar by sea is 1,050 nautical miles: from Gibraltar to Malta, 980; from Malta to Port Said, 940 miles. Cyprus is nearly 1,000 miles distant from Malta, and 250 from Port Said.

The Suez Canal.

We pass from the waters of the Mediterranean to those of the Red Sea through the famous Suez Canal, which was cut about twenty years ago through the sands of Egypt. This canal was planned by a celebrated French engineer, M. de Lesseps, and its construction was largely the result of French enterprise. Nevertheless, because Britain is a great trading and colonising country, she has gained much more advantage from the Canal than France or any other country. Much the largest part of the vast quantities of merchandise which are constantly passing through it is carried by British ships and owned by

FIG. 1. THE SUEZ CANAL.

N

British merchants.   Of the steamships which go through
it every year, about seventy-eight out of every hundred
carry the British flag.

The canal has therefore become for British commerce
the most important piece of water in the world outside of
our own home waters.   Its construction has greatly
changed our relations with many parts of the Empire.
For all purposes of trade and intercourse it has brought
Australia, India, and other places in the eastern and
southern seas much closer to England than they were
before.

Steamships from these places can now save many days
in coming to England compared with what could be done
when they had to go round the Cape of Good Hope or
Cape Horn.

The Indian and Australian mails therefore come and go
by this route.   So also do the large numbers of soldiers
whom we are constantly sending to or bringing back from
India.

The Canal is likewise the nearest line of communication with our newer settlements in East Africa.   Great
steamships are constantly passing from the Red Sea into
the Mediterranean, laden with the productions of India and
China—tea, coffee, silks, cotton, spices, gums, dyes, ivory,
precious stones, or with Australian wool, gold, silver,
lead, or tin.   They are met by others coming from the
Mediterranean into the Red Sea, laden with every kind
of British manufacture which our own people require
in India or Australasia, or which are used in trade
with the native races in the East.   The Canal is the

great meeting-place for the trade of the East and the West.

From **Port Said**, where the Canal is entered from the Mediterranean, to **Suez**, on the Red Sea, the distance is 87 miles. In this distance lakes, which required little or no excavation to make them deep enough for the passage of large ships, extend over 21 miles. The depth of the canal is 26 feet. At intervals of a few miles it is made of double width, and here ships going in one direction are moored, while those going in the opposite direction pass by them. Vessels are only allowed to steam at a slow speed, and the average time spent in the passage is now a little more than twenty hours.

The Passage through the Canal.

The navigation goes on by night as well as by day. On entering the canal for a night passage, each ship is provided with a powerful electric light. A very striking sight it is to see a long procession of great steamships coming through the canal, each with its brilliant light at the bow piercing far out into the desert gloom, and meeting a like procession, similarly illuminated, coming in the opposite direction. Less peculiar, but equally interesting, is the passage by day, when it is possible to realise how immense was the task of opening up this great channel through the desert. Excavation works are still usually going on, sometimes with dredges, sometimes by means of camels, which descend the banks, and kneel to have the panniers upon their backs filled with sand, which is then carried away, to be deposited at a distance from the canal.

Far as the eye can reach on either side stretches the
sandy or stony desert, with an occasional clump of palm-
trees or tuft of thorn-bush. Along the banks, almost the
only objects of interest are the trim little station-houses,
with their signalling apparatus of black balls upon flag-
staffs ; now and then a group of Arabs, with their camels ;
and the Egyptian flamingoes and pelicans, which stand
in long rows by the edges of the shallow pools or bitter
lakes.

Frenchmen deserve the highest praise for the skill
and energy which enabled them to plan and excavate
this great canal, so useful to the commerce* of the
world. British people, who have reaped such advantages
from the canal, should not forget to whom its construction
is due.

The Value of the Canal.

The use that we make of the Suez Canal for the vast
trade of the Empire causes our people in Australia and
India to be as much interested in its safety as the
people of Britain themselves.

* The canal is owned and managed by the Suez Canal Company. In this company, however, the British Government is now
the largest shareholder, having paid in 1875 nearly £4,000,000 sterling
for 176,602 shares previously possessed by the Khedive of Egypt.
The profit derived from working the canal in 1887 was £1,199,539,
and the interest paid to the shareholders amounted to 15·6 per cent.
3,389 vessels passed through the canal in 1890. Of the entire
number, the division among the various countries was as follows: —
English, 2,522 ; German, 275 ; French, 169 ; Dutch, 144 ; Italian, 87 ;
Austro-Hungarian, 55 ; Norwegian, 43 ; Spanish, 34 ; Turkish, 21 ;
Russian, 20 ; Portuguese, 7 ; Japanese, 4 ; Greek, 3 ; United States of
America, 3 ; Brazilian, 1 ; Siamese, 1.

If, for instance, Australian wool could not pass through the canal safely, the wool-growers in Australia would suffer as much loss as the wool-spinners in Yorkshire; and the same is true of other productions and manufactures passing between Britain and India or Australia. It would be for the common interest of our people in all these countries to use their united strength and influence to keep this great channel of trade safe and open at all times.

It is the existence of common interests like these which helps to bind a nation together.

Again, the canal gives the British nation a great interest in the good government of **Egypt**—the country through which it passes. So great is this interest, that when the Egyptian army rebelled against its Government in 1882, a British force was sent to put down the rebellion, and restore the power of the Khedive, as the ruler of the country is called. Since that time we have "occupied" Egypt: that is, we keep a small army there to assist the Egyptian forces in maintaining order and resisting the attacks of their chief enemies, the Arabs of the Soudan. Besides this, a number of English officials remain in Egypt to advise and assist the Khedive in the government of the country, and especially in the management of the taxes, of the courts of justice, and of the irrigation works.

Thus we have made ourselves responsible for the safety and good government of a country which is not our own, and we have done this chiefly on account of our interest in the safety of the Suez Canal.

Aden.

The fortified harbour of **Aden** watches over the month of the Red Sea, as Gibraltar does over the mouth of the Mediterranean, and is one of the most important of that line of protected coaling stations which connects Britain with Australia and the East. The territory which we possess at Aden includes an area of about 70 square miles. The harbour is excellent, but it is impossible to imagine anything more desolate and forbidding than the country which surrounds it. It is thus described by one who has visited it :—

FIG. 49.—ADEN.

"All around, above, about is hard, arid, barren, volcanic rock, calcined, contorted, ejected from ancient earth furnaces, and everywhere exhibiting the dry drear colours of extreme heat, brick-red sulphurous yellow, Tartarean black. A faint green tint here and there in the clefts of the sterile hills, where infrequent rain has trickled and dust has lodged, manifests the presence of sparse thorn-bushes and of the Aden lily, a pretty white-flowering bulb, which is well-nigh the only growing thing redeeming the utter desolation of the landscape."*

The intense heat of the summer months makes the

* Sir Edwin Arnold.

station a very trying one for English constitutions. During many months of every year, and sometimes for two or three years together, no rain falls, and artificial means have to be employed to secure a supply of water. In the hollows of the hills immense tanks, lined with cement, have been constructed, capable of holding many million gallons of rain-water, while condensing-engines are used to distil fresh water from the sea. Wells dug to a great depth in the rock, and an aqueduct from the mainland, furnish a small additional supply of brackish water.

In spite of all these difficulties, we have made of Aden an almost impregnable fortress. By excavating and tunnelling the volcanic rocks, batteries of heavy guns have been placed in position to command the approaches to the harbour, and we maintain there at all times a considerable body of British and native Indian troops. While Aden is chiefly valuable as a coaling station and as a place of safety for our ships, it is also the centre of a large and growing trade with Arabia and the neighbouring coast of Africa. **Coffee, spices, gums, hides, ivory, feathers,** and other products, are brought here to be shipped to England and other parts of the world.

No stranger mixture of nationalities could be seen anywhere in the Empire than in the streets of Aden. Europeans of every nation from the ships constantly calling at the port mingle with Arabs, Egyptians, negroes from the Somali coast, from Zanzibar and from Central Africa, Turks, Jews, Lascars, and the Indian merchants who carry on much of the trade of the place.

Perim and Socotra.

Along with Aden must be mentioned **Perim**, an island situated immediately in the Strait of **Bab-el-Mandeb**, and so commanding the entrance to the Red Sea at its narrowest point. It is a volcanic rock, with an area of about five square miles. Here we keep a small garrison of Indian troops; but beyond the fact that it has a lighthouse, the island is of little use except in the event of war, when its position, and the fact that it has an excellent harbour, would make its possession a matter of considerable importance.

In order to still further secure our position at the mouth of the Red Sea, the large island of **Socotra** was, by an agreement with its ruler, the sheikh of the neighbouring African coast, annexed to the Empire in 1886. No steps have as yet been taken to occupy the island, and its annexation was probably effected in order that it might not be taken possession of by any other Power.

Our possessions at the mouth of the Red Sea are all under the control of the Government of Bombay, and are looked upon as a part of British India. Their maintenance is therefore not a charge upon the revenues of the United Kingdom.

CHAPTER XVII.

INDIA.

The Road to India.

WE have now seen how great a hold the Empire has upon the vast continent of **Africa**. Beginning in the south, we have studied the great inland territories of Africa which are under the British flag, and have glanced at the smaller colonies which lie on or near its western shore. We then came round to the famous sea which washes the northern coast of Africa, and learnt how in the Mediterranean Britain has a great protected highway to the East. We saw how **Gibraltar**, **Malta**, **Aden**, and **Perim** were all sentinels upon a far-stretching road : that road is the one that brings us to India. It is to this great Empire of **India** that we have now come, and to which we must devote our attention.

India.

In **India**, we have come to a part of the Empire which may well be considered more wonderful than any which we have visited before. Here there are under British rule no less than 291,000,000 of people—that is, about one-sixth of the whole population of the globe, and more than seven times the number of people in our own British islands.

The area of the country we thus rule over is about eleven times that of the United Kingdom, or larger than the whole of Europe, if we leave out Russia.

In India we find numbers of great cities, some

containing nearly a million of inhabitants. We find harbours crowded with ships, mostly British, which carry on
an immense trade with other parts of the world. We see
magnificent temples, built in ancient times at enormous

FIG. 59.—INDIA, BURMAH, AND CEYLON.

expense, and splendid palaces, in which Indian princes and
emperors once lived. We find provinces far more densely
crowded with inhabitants than almost any other part of
the Empire. India is indeed a very wonderful land. No
other country except our own has ever in the history of
the world ruled over a dependency so vast as this, with a

population so numerous. How we got possession of it, and how we keep it, are things every Englishman ought to know something about.

The English in India.

That we do keep it will seem more wonderful when we reflect upon the fact that among all the 286,000,000 of inhabitants in the country, only about 150,000 are of British birth : that is, there is only one Englishman for nearly 2,000 of the natives. Besides this, the climate is not a good one for white people. English children cannot grow up there healthy and strong as they do here in England, and so have usually to be sent home by their parents at an early age. In many parts the heat is so great that Europeans must remove in the summer to the mountains to preserve their health. Most English people who go to India only stay a few years, and then come back to live in this country. In spite of all these things India has long been a part of the Empire, and is likely to remain under our rule.

The Population of India.

There are some facts which must be known about the population of the country before you can understand how English people got India, or how and why they keep it. The people of India never did, and do not now, form a single nation, belonging to the same race and speaking the same language, as is the case with such European nations as the Italians, French, or Spaniards. They belong to many different races, they speak more than a hundred different languages or dialects, and they have several distinct forms of religion. It is quite as incorrect to speak or think of India as a single nation as it would be to speak or think thus of the continent of Europe. India has been thus described :—*

"There you find **Hindoos, Mohammedans, Buddhists, Christians, Parsees,** and worshippers of the sun and moon, living side by side. You find not fewer varieties of language than in Europe, but more, only spoken in the same streets. You find race hatreds as violent as between Frenchmen and Germans, only between people who are meeting one another every hour of the day. Even the Hindoos, the largest of the native races, are not united. They are split up into "**castes**," by which certain occupations are hereditary. A member of a superior caste, such as a priest or a soldier, will consider himself polluted if he touch a vessel out of which one of an inferior caste has drunk. Between the Mohammedans, too, are religious differences as great as these, and it is impossible to point to any important section of the people of India who are united in blood, in language, and in religion."

The History of Divided India.

This remarkable condition of things arose chiefly from the circumstance that time after time India has been conquered by races who came from the mountainous regions and table-lands to the north and west. Some bold and adventurous leader would over-run the country

* "Our Colonies and India." By Prof. Cyril Ransome. Cassell & Company.

with his bands of warriors, and establish a vast empire to leave to his successors. They in their turn would yield to some new conqueror. Thus for hundreds of years before Englishmen arrived in the country India had been chiefly governed by foreign rulers. If we keep these facts in mind, it will be easier to understand how we were able to get possession of the country.

The East India Company.

Englishmen got their first footing in India as traders. In the year 1600 a number of merchants joined themselves together, and obtained a **Charter** from the English Government to carry on trade in India, just as charters are now given to companies to trade in different parts of Africa, in Borneo, and other places. This **East India Company**, as it was called, had at first no intention of conquering India or any part of it, but merely sent out agents, who established trading stations at various points, renting or buying the ground for their warehouses from the native princes, to whom they were subject. For more than a hundred years the company confined its attention entirely to trade, and took no part in the political affairs of India.

English and French in India.

As the Indian trade was profitable, the merchants of other nations were naturally anxious to secure a part of it for themselves. The Portuguese and Dutch had been in India before us, but the French, who came later, were our most serious rivals. With them for many years the East India Company, usually supported more or less by the

British Government, carried on a keen contest. At first it seemed likely that the French, under their great leader, **Dupleix**, would be successful, and had support been sent from France, a French Empire might have been founded in India. But the English Company at that time had the good fortune to have in its service **Robert Clive**, a man of remarkable ability both as a soldier and a ruler. Clive, who may be regarded as the founder of our Empire in India, by winning the famous battle of **Plassey** in 1757, got control of Bengal, the richest province in India. In 1760, the French, who had stirred up the Nabob of Bengal against us, were themselves utterly defeated in the battle of **Wandewash**, and in 1761 their strongest fortress, **Pondicherry**, was captured. It was not long after this that they were driven almost entirely out of the country, leaving the English Company free to spread its influence over India without European interference.

India as we found It.

Now, at that time the condition of the country was such as to greatly hinder the progress of trade and industry. This is how a distinguished writer describes the state of affairs :—

" When we began to take possession of the country, it was already in a state of wild anarchy such as Europe has perhaps never known. What government it had was pretty invariably despotic, and it was generally in the hands of military adventurers, depending on a soldiery composed of bandits whose whole vocation was plunder. The **Mahratta Power** covered the greater part of India, . . .

and yet this power was but an organisation of pillage."*
In this state of things, when the country which had been
conquered so often was split up into many States and
among many races all struggling for the mastery, we
cannot wonder that it occurred to some of those who
controlled the affairs of the East India Company that it
would be well if English rule could be extended so as
to establish the peace and order which are necessary for
prosperous trade. They thought, too, that there were
means by which it could be done.

Sepoys.

We often see soldiers or volunteers being drilled
hour after hour and day after day in order that they
may perform military duties well, and we know that
a man is not thought to be worth much as a soldier
till he has had this drill. Now, both the French and
English had noticed in India that a small body of
well-drilled European soldiers was more than a match
for many times its number of the untrained troops of
the native princes. These princes themselves had found
out the same thing, and so in the wars they carried on
with each other they often offered large sums of money
and much territory in return for the aid of French
or English troops. It had also been found that
European officers could drill native Indians into being
good soldiers. More than this, the natives of one race
were quite willing to enlist and fight under English or

* Prof. Seeley. " Expansion of England "

French orders against those of other races. So the practice was begun of hiring "**Sepoys**," as the native soldiers
are called, and giving them the best discipline possible.
The superior courage and discipline of British troops and
the employment of trained Sepoys were, then, the means
by which the East India Company gradually spread its
control over India during the hundred years after the
French were driven out. At Plassey, Robert Clive, with
1,000 English soldiers and 3,000 Sepoys, defeated more
than 40,000 followers of the Nabob of Bengal. The
same thing has been repeated many times in Indian
history

India under the Company.

For various reasons the Company was constantly compelled to interfere in the affairs of the native States.
Sometimes the quarrels of these States with each other
checked the Company's trade; sometimes they were com-
bining with each other or making treaties with the French
to expel the English from India. When the Company
did interfere, its well-trained troops and its command of
the sea gave it such an advantage that district after district,
province after province, and finally whole kingdoms, fell
in succession under its rule.

India under the Crown.

But it is not the East India Company which now
governs India. It is the **British people** themselves, who
do so through the **King** and **Parliament**. How did
this change came about? The Company was, as has
been said, merely a body of merchants trading for

gain. The men who were sent out to manage its affairs were often persons of great ability, and disposed to rule wisely and justly. Sometimes, however, one of them was tempted to use his power to make unjust gains for himself or the Company. When cases of this kind became known in England, Parliament began to insist on taking a large share in the government of India. It appointed the Governors-General and the Councils which assisted them, and it took steps to establish the **Indian Civil Service.** The members of this service, judges, magistrates, tax-collectors, and other officials, confined themselves to the task of governing the country, and were not allowed to have anything to do with trade, so that they had no temptation to use the natives unfairly. Under this system the government of the East India Company was much improved. But a much greater change was yet to come.

The Sepoy Mutiny.

We have seen how India was conquered for us largely by the help of native troops, or Sepoys. These same Sepoys proved, however, to be a great danger as well as a great assistance. In 1857 occurred the Sepoy Mutiny, when great numbers of the men whom we had drilled and armed so carefully rose in rebellion against our rule. There were frightful massacres of our people. For a short time it seemed probable that British power in India would be overthrown. Had the whole of the people of India joined in the rebellion, this would no doubt have taken place. But they did not do so, and of the Sepoys themselves many regiments remained faithful, and helped us to fight the

G

mutineers. The **Sikhs** of the Punjaub, whom we had conquered shortly before, fought valiantly upon the British
side, and rendered great assistance, as did also the princes
and people of some of the feudatory native States. The
common people of the country went on as usual rendering
us those services which are almost necessary for the existence of Europeans in the hot climate of India. Never
perhaps did British soldiers display greater courage and
endurance than during the Sepoy Mutiny. But it was
put down by native aid as well as by the exertions of our
own troops. The mutiny proved that India was not, and
probably never will be, a country which can be united
to oppose our rule.

The Empress of India.

The Mutiny of 1857 was followed by the important
change in the method of government to which reference
has been made. Our people had gradually made up their
minds that the East India Company, wonderful as was
the work which it had done in building up our Indian
Empire, was not a body suited for carrying on its government. By a Bill passed through Parliament in 1858, the
government of India was transferred from the Company
to the Sovereign, as the representative of the people of
this country. In 1877 Queen Victoria took the title of
Empress of India. Since 1858 the English people have
been entirely responsible, through the Sovereign and
Parliament, for the good government of our fellow-subjects
in India. How this work is carried on we shall briefly
explain in another place.

CHAPTER XVIII.

PHYSICAL FEATURES OF INDIA.

Geography of India.

LET us now consider the main features in the geography of the immense country which has thus been brought under English rule.

We see on the map that the greater part of India consists of a large peninsula, in shape something like a triangle, one side washed by the **Arabian Sea,** another by the **Bay of Bengal,** while on the north the vast range of the **Himalaya Mountains** forms an irregular base. The greatest length and greatest breadth are each about 1,900 miles.

The whole of this vast peninsula may be roughly divided into three sections :—

1. The mountainous region of the north, where the Himalayas, and the ranges which branch from them, gradually sink from far above the limit of perpetual snow to the hot plains beneath.

2. The great river plains, beginning at the foot of the Himalayas, extending east and west from sea to sea, and including the vast regions watered in the west by the Indus and its branches, and those on the east watered by the Ganges and Bramahpootra.

3. The Southern Peninsula, or Deccan, consisting chiefly of a great table-land bounded on the north by the Vindhya Mountains, and on its other sides by the Eastern and Western Ghauts.

The Mountain Region.

The **Himalayas** form the loftiest and grandest mountain range in the world. For many hundreds of miles they serve as a great wall of defence for India on the north, as they cannot be crossed by an army. But in the north-west is the famous **Khyber Pass**, an opening through which many invaders have come, and which we now guard with the greatest care.

The Himalayas also serve to collect, and in their higher regions of ice and snow to store up, the water which supplies the great rivers of India, upon which the prosperity and even the lives of more than 150,000,000 of people depend. As the **Indus** and **Bramahpootra** both rise to the north of the Himalayas, the water from both the northern and southern slopes is thus carried through the plains of India.

Between the summits of these great mountains, the highest peak of which, **Mount Everest**, is more than 29,000 feet high, and the hot plains beneath, are found all the climates of the world, with most of the productions of the Arctic, temperate and tropical zones.

The River Plains.

Southwards from the Himalayas lie the great river plains. Here are to be found the richest, most populous, and most prosperous parts of India.

On the west, the **Indus**, 1,800 miles long, flowing from behind the Himalayas, receives the waters of the **Jhelum, Chenab, Ravee,** and **Sutlej,** from the southern slopes of those mountains.

These rivers give the district its name of Punjaub, or "Five Rivers." The Indus system drains an area of over 300,000 square miles.

The **Ganges**, though only about 1,600 miles long, drains the still larger area of 500,000 square miles, and is

FIG. 51.—CALCUTTA.
(*From a photograph by Frith & Co., Reigate.*)

by far the most important river of India. As it approaches the sea it is joined by the **Bramahpootra**, 1,500 miles long. An immense delta, called the **Sunderbunds**, and itself nearly as large as Ireland, has been formed at their mouths by the mud brought down from the Hima-layas.

The fertility of these river plains, especially that of the Ganges, is very great. They sustain a population of

more than 150,000,000 of people. In Lower Bengal
there are three harvests each year; pease, pulse, and
various oil seeds are reaped in April and May, the early

FIG. 52.—BENARES.

rice crop in September, and the great rice crop two or
three months later.

Along the valley of the Ganges is a wonderful succession of great cities: **Delhi, Agra, Cawnpore, Lucknow,**

Allahabad, Benares, Mirzapur, Patna, Dacca, and **Calcutta,** with innumerable smaller towns and villages.

The Deccan

The table-land of the **Deccan** is surrounded on all sides by mountains. Its average elevation above the sea is between 2,000 and 3,000 feet.

On the eastern and western coasts, between the mountains and the sea, are narrow strips of flat fertile country, much given up to the cultivation of rice.

Bombay, on the west coast, is the largest city, and one of the great seaports of the world. When the American War in 1861-5 cut off the mills of Lancashire from supplies of American cotton, they had to obtain it from India, and Bombay became one of the chief cotton markets in the world. About 1,000,000 cwts. are now exported every year, while half as much more is spun and woven in the country.

Madras, on the east coast, is also a city of great importance.

Burmah.

The great province of **Burmah,** which lies eastward of the Indian Peninsula, still remains to be mentioned.

Until a few years ago our possessions in Burmah consisted of a narrow strip of the coast of Further India, stretching along the Bay of Bengal. In 1886 **Upper Burmah** was annexed. The province now contains 280,000 square miles, and is the largest in British India.

The inland parts are mountainous, covered with forests, and only in parts suited for agriculture. On the

flat and fertile lands of the coast are raised immense
quantities of rice, which is the chief product of the
country, about £6,000,000 worth being exported every year.
A great deal is sent to England, as well as to America,
China, and the continent of Europe. The forests supply
teak, valuable for ship-building, and other woods. The
ruby mines are the most famous in the world, and there
are also mines of silver, copper, tin, lead, and coal.

Our possession of Burmah seems likely to open up for
us a new and large field for commerce outside of the
country itself. The river Irrawaddy is navigable for 200
miles, to a point not far from the frontiers of China. It
is proposed to construct from this point a railway into
China, and so have a short route for carrying on trade
with a large and thickly populated region.

Rangoon and Mandalay are the chief towns of
Burmah.

Ceylon.

For convenience sake we may here give a description
of the island of Ceylon, which, as will be seen on the map,
lies like a pearl-drop at the extremity of the great Indian
Peninsula. Though geographically a part of India, however, Ceylon is not under the Indian Government, but is
treated as a colony by itself under the Colonial Office.
For this reason we must make a distinction between what
is said of the Government of India and Burmah on the
one hand, and that of Ceylon on the other.

Ceylon is a beautiful and commercially valuable
island. Its length from north to south is 266 miles,
its greatest breadth 140 miles, and its size is more than

three-fourths that of Ireland. The inhabitants number more than 3,500,000.

The Portuguese, who were the first Europeans to occupy the country, kept it chiefly under their influence for more than a century. In 1658 they were expelled by the Dutch, who retained it till 1796, when they in their turn gave it up to an English force. Since that time it has been governed as a Crown colony of the Empire.

The products which Ceylon sends to our English markets are very important. The early traders were attracted by its **spices**, of which quantities are still exported. Chief among these is **cinnamon**, which grows here in greater perfection than in any other part of the world. Between two and three millions of pounds are produced every year, and nearly 50,000 acres of land are devoted to its cultivation.

Far more important is the culture of **tea, coffee, and cinchona bark**. It is in the management of the plantations on which these are grown that the English settlers in Ceylon are chiefly engaged. For many years coffee planting was the leading and most profitable industry. About fifteen years ago a disease attacked the coffee plants, which spread so rapidly that many planters were almost ruined. With great energy they turned to the cultivation of **tea**. The result has been very wonderful, and is a striking example of what British capital and energy can do when it is turned in any direction. In 1878 Ceylon was sending us no tea. In 1889, only eleven years later, it sent us half as much as we received from China, so long the great centre of the tea trade. In 1901 the export was 144,275,608 pounds weight, and the production is still rapidly increasing. The quality of the tea, also, is considered by many much superior to that of China.

The bark of the cinchona tree furnishes the **quinine** which is so much used in medicine. This tree, originally a native of South America, has been introduced into Ceylon and India with great success. A large quantity of bark is now exported annually from Ceylon.

The tea, coffee, and cinchona plantations are all cultivated chiefly by native labour, and so Ceylon does not offer a field for emigration so much as for the employment of English money and English skill in producing by native help many things which this country requires.

Rice is the chief food of the native population, and about 600,000 acres are given up to its cultivation. Next in importance is the cocoa-nut palm, groves of which fringe all the coasts of Ceylon. The variety of uses to which the different parts of this tree are put is so great that it seems capable of supplying nearly all the wants of the natives. It gives them food and drink, timber for their boats and houses, materials for thatching, for manufacturing mats, cordage, baskets, and domestic utensils; while the nuts themselves, oil from the kernel, and coir fibre, are largely exported.

Ceylon has for ages been famous for its **precious stones**. It has no diamonds like South Africa, but parts of the island are rich in **rubies, sapphires, cat's-eyes,** and other gems. The **pearl** fishery on the north-west coast is one of the most valuable and productive in the world.

It yields a considerable revenue to the Government, to which it belongs. Among useful minerals **plumbago** is the most important. Large quantities of this are supplied to English markets.

Colombo is the capital. The construction of a splendid breakwater has made it a good harbour and coaling station. **Trincomalee**, on the north-east coast, has also an excellent harbour, which, like that of Colombo, is being strongly fortified. **Galle**, a port of call on the south coast, and **Kandy**, in the interior, are other towns.

The **Maldives** are a group of islands in the Indian Ocean tributary to Ceylon.

●●●

CHAPTER XIX.

BRITISH RULE IN INDIA.

The Defence of India.

To defend this vast country of India and to maintain our power there, we have an army of about 200,000 men. Of these, some 70,000 are British troops, while the native soldiers are more than double that number. To carry on the ordinary work of government there are about three thousand officials belonging to the Civil Service.

It should be remembered that the government and defence of India do not cost British people anything. The **Viceroy**, Governors, Judges, and other officials of various kinds, the officers and soldiers of the army, whether

British or native, are all paid out of the taxes of India itself. So, too, in the construction of Indian railways, canals, public buildings, and other national works, the people of this country take no burden upon themselves. Even the expense of defending Aden, so important to the whole nation as a coaling and naval station, is borne by the Indian people.

On the other hand, India pays nothing directly into the revenue of Great Britain. When Rome had conquered and ruled over the greater part of the ancient world, each province was expected to pay a certain amount into the imperial revenue, that the taxes of Roman people might be diminished. Spain compelled Mexico, Peru, the West India Islands, and other provinces which she had conquered, to pay her in the same way large sums in tribute. We have adopted the different plan of having all public money raised in India spent on India itself.

It may be thought that because Great Britain pays nothing for the defence and government of India, and receives nothing from it in the form of taxes, that therefore from a money point of view it makes no difference to us whether we possess it or not.

It would be a very great mistake to think this, and it can easily be shown that the comfort and prosperity of great numbers of people in this country depend in various ways on our possession and government of India.

Indian Trade.

Let us first look at the trade question. Every year the people of these islands sell to India more than

£30,000,000 worth of manufactured goods. In the year
1901 India took cotton goods and yarns alone to the value
of £21,650,000, or almost a third of all that was exported
from the whole of this country. We can see, then, how
much the manufacturers and work-people of a great
cotton-spinning county like Lancashire depend for work
and prosperity upon having such a market as this in which
to sell their goods.

In the same way, many millions of pounds' worth
of **machinery, hardware, railway iron, woollens,** and
other goods, are sent every year from the factories of
Yorkshire, Scotland, and other parts of these islands to
India.

In return for these goods, India sends us nearly
£30,000,000 worth of **wheat, rice, tea, coffee, raw cotton,
jute, hides, indigo, wool,** and other products, which furnish
to our people either food or the material which they use in
manufacture.

We shall find later that the power of the Indian people
to supply us with these products or to buy our goods
depends very much upon our government of their
country.

From these facts we may more easily understand what
Lord Dufferin meant when he said, in a speech to the
merchants of London, that—" It would not be too much
to say that if any serious disaster ever overtook our
Indian Empire, or if our political relations with the
Peninsula of Hindostan were to be even partially dis-
turbed, there is not a cottage in Great Britain—at all
events in the manufacturing districts—which would not

be made to feel the disastrous consequences of such an intolerable calamity."

India's Tribute to Britain.

But British people receive from India a great deal more than what they get from commerce.

It has been estimated that the United Kingdom draws no less than sixty or seventy million pounds a year from India in direct payments. This comes to us in different forms. Part consists in the pay of the British officers and soldiers, of whom so many thousands serve in the Indian army, and whose pay is much better than when they are serving at home. Several thousands of Englishmen also receive well-paid employment in carrying on the government of the country, as governors, collectors, judges, magistrates, engineers, clerks, and so on. Then an enormous amount of British money—some hundreds of millions sterling—is employed in the construction of Indian railways, canals, and other public works, and in carrying on Indian industries. The interest or profit of this money comes to Britain; and we may be quite sure that there are a great many thousands of people in these islands who depend for their living on money which in one way or another comes to them from India.

If another nation, such as Russia, should conquer India, and take it from us, or if we left the country, and it fell back into the disorder which prevailed when we began to rule it, almost all these sources of income, which make so many of our people comfortable and prosperous, would disappear.

What Britain does for India.

On the other hand, British rule has done a great deal for India. We can truly say that British people now wish to govern India for the good of the people in it. So we send out many of our ablest public men to make and carry out just laws, and they have given to the country peace, order, and justice, such as it knew little about in old times. Of all our exports to India none are so valuable to the country as the honest and upright men which we have sent to it.

Many things have been done to greatly increase the prosperity of the country. Nearly 20,000 miles of railway have been built, opening up communication, and enabling the people of the remote districts to send to market the commodities which they produce for sale. It is found that as more railways are constructed, the imports and exports largely increase, showing that the people are able to buy more and produce more.

Even more important than railways is the system of irrigation canals which has been made under our direction. We should note why these are so much needed and do so much good.

Famine.

One of the greatest dangers which the dense population of India has always had to fear is that of famine. We hear of terrible famines, in which millions of people perished from want of food long before Britain had much to do with the country, and even under our government there has sometimes been a great loss of life from the same cause. It is well that we should understand why this danger is so great in India.

There are facts about our own country which will help to make the condition of India clear.

If all the inhabitants of England and Wales were distributed evenly over the whole country, it is estimated that there would be nearly 450 in each square mile. It requires immense quantities of food to supply so many people. We have a climate which is generally favourable for agriculture, and crops seldom entirely fail. Even so, however, we do not produce in England nearly all the food required by our dense population. We get from other countries great supplies of corn, flour, meat, cheese, sugar, and many other articles of food. Fortunately, we are able to pay for these with the manufactured goods which millions of our people are engaged in making. If seasons be bad and crops poor, we import more provisions from abroad, and so avoid the risk of famine.

Now, there are large areas of India where the population is even denser than in England and Wales. Taking the whole vast country together, there is the high average of 167 persons to each square mile, which is much higher than the average in Scotland or Ireland.

The people depend almost entirely on the productions of the soil, not only for their own food, but for what they export to other countries. The climate is one which at times causes severe droughts, occasionally followed by excessive rains. When the crops fail their main support is gone. At such periods millions of people, if left unaided, may be reduced to starvation. No words could picture the terrible misery and suffering which have thus been caused in India.

Even in this country something of the same kind has been known, for Ireland has occasionally suffered severely from famine. There the people in some large districts have been accustomed to depend chiefly on the potato crop for food. When this crop failed in 1845, great numbers of people died before help could be brought to them, either from actual starvation or from disease brought on by want of proper nourishment. Even now there is occasionally danger that from a similar cause there may be a scarcity of food in the poorer districts of Ireland.

The chief cause of Indian famines is drought. The rains fail to come at the usual season, and then the crops are destroyed by the heat. Now, the only way to meet this danger is by irrigation.

At very great expense canals have been constructed, which lead away the water from all the large rivers, and distribute it over the district which suffers from drought. There are now more than 14,000 miles of these canals in different parts of India, which supply water to many millions of acres of land, and so make the country more capable of supplying the wants of its people.

Our Good Work in India.

In many other ways the condition of the people has been improved. Some of the worst evils of heathenism, such as the custom of burning widows with the dead bodies of their husbands, and the murder of little children by their own parents, once very common practices, have

P

been put down. Now a great deal of attention is being
given to education, and large numbers of colleges and

FIG. 53.—THE "MAN IN THE RED COAT."

schools have been established. In these and other ways
British people are striving to make their rule of India a
good thing for its inhabitants.

The "Man in the Red Coat."

Before we leave the subject of India altogether, we
must say one word more about a very important individual
who must on no account be forgotten. We have spoken

of the Viceroy or Governor-General, of the Officers of
State, of the Civil Service, and of all the wise and able
men whom Britain sends out to govern her great Indian
Empire. These are men of whom the country has reason
to be proud, and to whose courage and judgment we owe it
in a great measure that we are able to retain our possessions
in India. But there is one other personage upon whom all
these others depend, and without whom we should un-
doubtedly have to give up all the good work which we are
now able to do in India. We have here a picture of the
man who, above all others, retains our rule in India, the
brave, patient, ever trustworthy " man in the red coat,"
the British private soldier. Here we see him marching
stolidly up and down on sentry outside one of the great
Indian palaces, doing his duty in peace as he is sure to do it
in war. The heroism and endurance of our soldiers in India
form a very bright page in the history of our country, and
when we are called upon to give honour where honour is due
to those who keep India for the British Crown, we must
put in a very high, if not the highest place, the " man in
the red coat."

The emblem of India is a very beautiful one. It is the
star which forms the decoration that has been chosen for the
Indian order of knighthood—the Order of the Star of
India, with its motto " Heaven's Light our Guide " ; it
may be seen on the bow of the great troopships which plough
the Mediterranean and the Indian Ocean with soldiers for
the army of India, and on the breast of many a distinguished soldier and public servant who has helped to win
or helped to keep our great Asiatic Empire.

CHAPTER XX.

THE NATIVE STATES OF INDIA.

British and Native States.

WE may now point out one or two facts about the way in which Government is carried on in India.

The first thing to remember is that the whole country is divided under two heads—*British Territory* and *Native States.*

The **British Territory** is that which is entirely under the control of our own English Government. This is by far the larger part, extending over more than a million square miles, and having a population of about 230,000,000 souls. It is divided into several great provinces, such as **Bengal, Bombay, Madras,** and the **Punjaub.** Over each province is a Governor, or Chief Commissioner, under whom are collectors and other officers in control of the districts into which a province is divided.

The mass of the people themselves have nothing to say in the appointment of these officials or in making the laws by which they are ruled. There are no elections in India of County Councillors or Members of Parliament to make laws or carry out the wishes of the people as there are in this country. Both those who frame the laws and those who carry them out are appointed to their posts—the more important ones by the King and Government of this country, and inferior officers, both English and native, by those thus sent out.

A different form of government prevails in the **Native States,** of which there are several hundreds scattered over

various parts of India, some large and populous, others
quite small communities. In all they contain a population
numbering not far from 65,000,000.

In these states the people are no more consulted than
in the British territory, but the administration of government is mainly in the hands of the native princes or chiefs.
A British agent or **Resident** is kept at each Court, and
affairs are usually managed with his advice or assistance.

These native rulers acknowledge the King as their
sovereign, and in some cases pay a fixed amount of money
to the Indian Government. They have no right to make
peace or war, and they agree not to maintain more than a
certain number of troops. When a native state has been
seriously misgoverned the Governor-General has sometimes dethroned its ruler and replaced him by another.

Thus it will be seen how wide a difference there
is between the government of a dependency like India,
and parts of the Empire like Canada or Australia. In
these great colonies the people choose men to manage
their affairs, impose their own taxes, and decide how
their money is to be spent. They govern themselves.
In India the people are governed. They had been accustomed to this for ages before we got possession of the
country. How much longer the same kind of rule will be
necessary it is impossible to say. In Eastern countries
changes come very slowly.

CHAPTER XXI.

BRITISH POSSESSIONS IN EASTERN SEAS.

Asiatic Colonies.

CLOSELY connected with our Indian Empire are the groups of islands which we possess in the Bay of Bengal and the settlements of the **Malay Peninsula.**

The **Andaman Islands,** off the coast of Burmah, are

FIG. 51.—EAST INDIAN SEA.

used as a convict settlement for British India. One of the **Nicobar Islands,** farther south, is used in the same way. Both groups of islands are heavily wooded. Their chief productions are cocoa-nuts, ambergris, and tortoise-shell.

Singapore.

The **Straits Settlements** is the name given to our possessions on the west and south coasts of the Malay Peninsula. The various settlements are grouped together into a Crown colony, which has rapidly grown into great commercial importance.

Singapore is by far the most important of the Straits Settlements. It is an island 27 miles long and 14 broad, having a population of about 225,000. The town of Singapore is the seat of government for the whole colony.

Singapore was ceded to the British Government in 1824 by the Sultan of Johore. It has now become one of the great centres of the world's commerce. Through it passes most of the trade of Europe with the far East, of the Dutch with their East Indian colonies, and of Australia with China and Japan.

Singapore has a splendid harbour, strongly fortified at the expense of the colony itself, only the heavy guns for the batteries being supplied by

FIG. 55.— THE STRAITS SETTLEMENTS.

the British Government. The harbour has miles of wharves with fine docks. From its relation to Eastern trade, Singapore is one of the most important points in the Empire. It is a free port, no duty being charged upon any goods which enter it.

Penang and Malacca.

Farther north is **Penang**, an island containing 107 square miles, which was ceded to the Government of India in 1786 by a native prince. It is the centre of a large and increasing trade with the neighbouring mainland and Sumatra.

The province of **Wellesley**, a small district on the coast of the peninsula, and the **Dindings**, which include some islands with another strip of coast, are governed from Penang.

Malacca is the largest of the Straits Settlements, and has an area of 659 square miles. It was first occupied by the Portuguese, who were driven out by the Dutch, from whom we captured it in 1795. Afterwards it was secured to Britain in 1824 by treaty, when we gave Holland in exchange for it our possessions in Sumatra.

Besides these settlements, which are entirely under the control of our Government, most of the remaining territory of the Malay Peninsula has been put under British protection by the native princes.

The peninsula comprises regions of great fertility, and its productions are of great importance to English commerce. They include **tin, sugar, rice, pepper, spices, dye-stuffs, guttapercha, indiarubber, tapioca, gums, and tobacco.**

The **Cocos Islands**, 700 miles west of Sumatra, are considered a part of the Straits Settlements, and one of the group has been used as a coaling station. The products of the cocoa-palm are the chief exports.

Borneo, Labuan, etc.

British North Borneo is another of those districts which have been handed over by a Royal Charter* to an English company to manage. It has an area of 31,000 square miles,

---

* *See* under South Africa, page 177.

with a population numbering 200,000. A large trade is carried on in products very similar to those of the Straits Settlements.

Labuan, on the north-west coast of Borneo, has large coal deposits. The mines, though not now worked to any considerable extent, may become of much importance. The island is managed by the British North Borneo Company.

Brunei is a native territory of Borneo, which has been taken under British protection.

Sarawak and Raja Brooke.

While speaking of our Eastern possessions, it is worth while to mention a very curious instance of success achieved by an Englishman in ruling a coloured race. On the western coast of the island of Borneo, south of the territory of Brunei, there is a large district called **Sarawak**. It is rather larger than Scotland, and has a population numbering 600,000. This district, though not a part of the Empire, is ruled by an Englishman, with the aid of a staff of English officers. About fifty years ago **Mr. James Brooke**, an English gentleman, who was sailing in his yacht around these seas, became interested in the country, and filled with a desire to better the condition of the uncivilised people. He succeeded in persuading the Sultan to make him a large grant of territory, and then proceeded to repress piracy, which was common on the coast, establish law and order, and encourage commerce. The people soon began to find that under his rule they were safer, happier, and more prosperous than they had ever been before, and so willingly submitted to and supported his power. As the English Government was unwilling to make Sarawak a part of the Empire, Raja Brooke, as he was commonly called, continued during his life to rule the country as an independent sovereign, maintaining a small army and navy, arranging taxes, and executing the laws which he had framed. He has now been succeeded in the government by his nephew. Most people will feel that one who earnestly tried, as Raja Brooke did, to rule for the good of those he governed, deserved the success and fame which he gained.

Hong-Kong.

Hong-Kong is a colony small in area, but of great commercial importance to the Empire, from the commanding

FIG. 56.—HONG-KONG.

position which it occupies in the China Sea. It is an island eleven miles long and from two to five miles broad,

FIG. 57. A QUIET STREET IN HONG-KONG.

situated just within the tropics, at the mouth of the Canton River, and ninety miles distant from the large Chinese city of **Canton.** Several small islets and a peninsula which juts into the harbour, with an area of four square miles, are also included in the colony. The island consists of a broken ridge of high hills, and contains very little ground fit for cultivation, its value depending chiefly upon its splendid harbour. This harbour has an area of about ten square miles, is sheltered on all sides by lofty hills, and is connected with the sea by two excellent channels, which are now protected by strong fortifications.

Hong-Kong has been in our possession about fifty years, having been ceded to the British Government after the Chinese war of 1841. At that time the island was little more than a barren rock, inhabited only by a few fishermen or pirates who frequented the surrounding waters. Now it has a population of over 283,000, and is the third port in the British Empire in respect of the tonnage of shipping entered and cleared every year. In 1901 this amounted to more than 7,000,000 tons.

Hong-Kong is the head-quarters of our China Squadron, and the centre of our great trade with China. In the harbour may usually be seen thousands of Chinese junks, which carry on commerce with the mainland. The larger proportion of the population consists of Chinese, who have become British subjects. It is from this port also that the emigration of Chinese coolies chiefly takes place, and an important part of the duty of the Government of the colony is to see that this emigration is carried on without injustice to the coolies.

Hong-Kong is a free port, and has thus become the emporium of trade between China and other nations, as well as ourselves. British steamship lines from England,

India, Canada, and Australia; American lines from San Francisco, German lines from the North Sea, and French lines from the Mediterranean, all meet here, and swell the trade of the port.

The town is a busy and interesting place.

" Well-to-do shops, both English and Chinese, line the streets on either side; substantial buildings of brick and granite attract the eye. Thick-leaved rows of banyan trees line the roads; an air of general activity conveys a sense of prosperity or contentment; while the spectator is amused by the bewildering confusion of jinrickshas, sedan-chairs, peripatetic cook stalls, pedestrians of all sorts, hawkers, barbers' stands, coolies carrying their nicely balanced loads on bamboos, women with children strapped on their backs, all making a motley crowd that fills the streets from morning to night. The aspect from the sea is of especial beauty, with something of the rugged grandeur of the Western Scottish Isles and a suggestion of Italian softness and grace."

New Guinea.

The great island of **New Guinea** has been divided into three parts—**British, Dutch,** and **German.** The British territory comprises 88,000 square miles, and extends over the south-east portion of the island. It was annexed in 1888, when the Australian colonies agreed to pay £15,000 a year towards the cost of its government. The native population, numbering perhaps 350,000, consists of a low type of savages. They have, however, very clear ideas about the ownership of their land, which is divided

among tribes and families. In the administration of the
country the native rights are respected, and as New Guinea
is not a country suited for European settlement, the
chief object aimed at in the occupation of the island is
the promotion of trade. The **Administrator** of the colony
acts under the direction of the Government of Queensland.

Mauritius.

When trade with India was carried on around the Cape
of Good Hope, **Mauritius** was a very important station for

FIG. 5.— MAURITIUS.

ships making the voyage between Europe and the East.
It was for some time held by the Dutch, but afterwards it
fell into the hands of the French, under whose care it
became a rich, populous, and important colony, under the
name of "**Isle of France**." In our wars with France at

the end of the eighteenth and the beginning of the nine-
teenth century, it was made a centre from which to attack
British commerce in the Indian Ocean. Its conquest was
therefore resolved upon, and this was effected in the year
1810. Thus in Mauritius, as in Canada, large numbers of
French people became, and have continued to be, British
subjects. There also, as in Canada, the French have been
allowed to retain their own laws and customs.

Mauritius is almost entirely given up to the cultivation
of the sugar-cane. Under the rule of France, and for
some time after the island came under the sway of Britain,
the labour of the sugar plantations was performed by
slaves. In 1835 slavery was abolished, and the planters
received £2,000,000 sterling as compensation from the
British Government.

The abolition of slavery led to the introduction of great
numbers of Indian "coolies," * as giving another form of
cheap coloured labour. These coolies, or their descendants,
now form by far the larger part of the population, numbering more than 250,000 out of the 370,000 inhabitants of
the island.

No colony of the Empire furnishes a more striking
example of the strangely mixed population which is sometimes found under British rule. Besides the comparatively
small number of English residents, there are the descendants of the old French settlers, the Creoles, or descendants
of both white and coloured parents, Indian coolies, African
negroes, Malays, Chinese, and natives of Madagascar and
Ceylon.

* See West Indies, chap. v.

English is the language used in the courts of law, but French is more generally spoken among the educated classes, while, as may be supposed, the language of the mass of the people is of a very mixed kind.

Besides sugar, which is its chief production, Mauritius exports rum, coffee, cocoa, vanilla, and a fibre known as "Mauritius hemp." Almost everything which the island produces is exported, and it has to procure from abroad nearly all the necessaries of life, both food and manufactured goods.

The Seychelles.

We find several groups of islands scattered through the Indian Ocean, as dependencies, under the government of Mauritius.

About 1,000 miles to the north of Mauritius are the Seychelles, consisting of twenty-nine islets. They, too, were originally settled by the French, and ceded to Britain in 1814. The whole group comprises about 50,120 acres, and has a population of about 19,000. The largest island is Mahé, which has an excellent harbour, at which steamships stop to coal on the passage from Aden to Mauritius and other ports. Cocoa-nut oil, cocoa, Indian corn, and vanilla are the chief products and exports. The scenery of the islands is very beautiful, the soil is fertile, and the climate is said to be better than that of any other tropical portion of the Empire.

Rodrigues.

Next to the Seychelles Islands in importance is the island of Rodrigues, situated 350 miles eastward from

Mauritius. It is 18 miles long and 7 broad, and has a population numbering more than 3,100. souls. It was taken possession of in 1810 by the British force which was preparing to capture Mauritius, and was of great service to that expedition. The chief industries are **fishing** and the rearing of **cattle** and **goats**. The soil is exceedingly fertile, producing **oranges, limes,** and **citrons** of excellent quality, and indeed all the fruits of the tropics. The want of regular communication with other places and a scarcity of labour discourage agriculture, for which the island is well adapted, and which flourished to a greater extent than now before the abolition of slavery.

Diego Garcia, one of the **Chagos Archipelago,** has of late years been used as a coaling station for steamships going between Aden and Australia.

CHAPTER XXII.

TRADE OF THE EMPIRE.

The Great Trade Routes of the Empire.

WE have mentioned before that there is scarcely any part of the ocean where trade is to be carried on in which British ships are not sometimes found. But there are certain lines over which they have to pass continually in carrying on the commerce of the Empire.

These are our great **trade routes,** which we shall now describe. It will be well to arrange them in a certain

Q

order, and number them, so that we can easily trace them
out on the map.

1. From England, by way of the Straits of Gibraltar,
through the Mediterranean, the Suez Canal, and the Red
Sea, into the Indian Ocean, and thence by the Straits of
Malacca into the China Sea.

2. The two Australian branches of this line from
Ceylon, one passing southward by King George's Sound,
along the southern coast of Australia, and the other along
the northern and eastern coasts, by way of the Java Sea
and Torres Straits.

3. From England, down the West Coast of Africa to
the Cape of Good Hope. Here this route separates into
two main lines, one branch going northward to the
Indian Seas, the other eastward to Australia and New
Zealand.

4. From Australia and New Zealand, and eastward
around Cape Horn, and then northward through the
Atlantic Ocean to England.

5. From Great Britain across the North Atlantic to
the St. Lawrence, Halifax, and other points on the coast
of North America.

6. From Great Britain to the West India Islands,
British Guiana, and Honduras. Should a canal be
made through the Isthmus of Panama, this line would
form a part of a new and short route to Australasia.

7. From British Columbia to Japan and Hong-Kong,
where a connection is made with the great Eastern routes.

8. From British Columbia southward through the
Pacific to New Zealand and Australia. This route, not

much used at present, is likely to become of great importance in the future.

9. From the eastern ports of Canada southward to the West India Islands.

These are the main lines along which British commerce flows. From them short branches reach almost every centre of trade within the Empire or in foreign countries. It is difficult even to conceive in the mind the value of the goods carried over these great trade routes. It has been estimated that in a single year more than £1,100,000,000 worth of merchandise belonging to British people is afloat upon the ocean.

How we Defend the Trade Routes.

We must now observe the positions which our nation holds along most of these great trade routes — positions which give us a singular advantage both for carrying on commerce and for defending it in time of need.

Along the first route to the East we possess **Gibraltar, Malta, Cyprus, Perim, Aden, Bombay, Colombo, Trincomalee, Singapore,** and **Hong-Kong** — all places which furnish harbours of refuge for ships, most of them strongly fortified, and some believed to be impregnable to attack.

Along the Cape of Good Hope route we have naval stations at **Sierra Leone, Ascension, St. Helena, Table Bay** and **Simon's Bay** (near the Cape), **Mauritius,** and one or two of the minor islands of the Indian Ocean.

In Australia there are harbours at **Melbourne, Sydney, King George's Sound, Brisbane, Thursday Island,** and **Port**

Darwin; in Tasmania, at **Hobart**; in New Zealand, at **Auckland, Wellington, Lyttelton,** and **Dunedin.**

Some of these Australasian harbours are among the best in the world; many are already strongly defended, and others are having important fortifications erected.

On the route round Cape Horn we possess the **Falkland Islands**, which furnish a port of call for ships.

For the great lines which cross the Atlantic we have the strongly fortified positions of **Quebec, Halifax, Bermuda,** and **Kingston,** in **Jamaica,** with other ports and coaling stations in Eastern Canada, Newfoundland, and the West Indies.

On the Pacific coast of Canada there are excellent harbours, and the important station of **Esquimalt** has been put into a state of defence, to protect trade at this terminus of the two Pacific routes.

Almost as important as the fortifications which defend these ports are the docks, which in many of them have been constructed at great expense for the repair of ships.

There are such docks at **Malta, Bombay, Hong-Kong, Sydney, Auckland, Lyttelton, Halifax, Esquimalt,** and **Bermuda,** and arrangements are being made for their construction at **Gibraltar** and other points.

Vessels which have been damaged by storms or in any other way can be taken into these docks and re-fitted so as to resume their voyages.

In time of war this can be done under the shelter of strong fortifications.

Coal and Coaling Stations.

We have spoken of some of the positions which we hold along the great trade routes as **coaling stations**, and the same term might rightly be applied to all of them. The importance of these places as coaling stations should be clearly understood.

We all know how useful coal is, and how much the comfort and prosperity of people in this country depend on the great supplies of it which are found in our mines. Coal warms our houses, cooks our food, and gives us the gas with which we light up our streets and homes. It drives the machinery by which are carried on the manufactories which give employment to millions of our people. It has often been truly said that Britain owes her wealth, which is greater than that of any other country, chiefly to her mines of coal.

We notice that every engine on the railways which convey passengers and goods in all directions over the country, has to carry a supply of coal for fuel, without which it would be useless.

So, too, at nearly every railway-station there are large piles of coal, from which the engines can get new supplies.

If we are near the docks of a great shipping port, like London, Liverpool, or Hull, we see wharves covered with immense quantities of coal, and whenever a steamship starts for some distant part of the world, a great deal is put into her hold to supply fuel for her engines. But though hundreds, and even thousands, of tons are thus often taken on board a single ship, still she cannot with her other freight carry enough for the long voyages which sometimes have to be taken. Just as the railway-engines have to get new supplies at the stations, so steamships must take in new supplies at intervals of a few thousands of miles.

In the last few years a very remarkable change has taken place in the kind of ships with which trade is chiefly carried on. The number of steamships has increased very much, and the number of sailing-vessels has diminished.* You will understand, then, that commerce must depend much more now upon coal and coaling stations than it did in the past. The change is still more striking in the case of ships of war. Sailing-vessels are now of little use for naval purposes, and are scarcely employed at all.

The result of all this is that large stores of coal must be kept at most of the ports which have been mentioned along the great trade routes. A great deal of this coal is raised from mines in the United Kingdom, and carried in ships to the places where it is wanted. Thus supplying our coaling stations gives employment to numbers of colliers in the English, Welsh, and Scotch mines, as well as to the sailors who carry the coal abroad.

The remote stations, however, do not depend on England for coal.

Coal on the Trade Routes.

In almost all the distant parts of the world where our

* For the five years ending in 1901 there was in the United Kingdom a decline of 1,339 in the number of sailing-vessels, and of 598,913 tons in the tonnage; and in steam-vessels an increase of 894 in the number, and 1,254,192 tons in the tonnage.

people have settled they have found great deposits of coal, which give the same advantage to industry and commerce that our own do here. Indeed, one of the most remarkable facts about our Empire is the way in which coal is distributed over its various parts, and in places where it is most useful to a great trading nation.

Let us once more glance over the map of the world, that we may learn the great advantage our nation enjoys in this way, and the relation of the larger coal deposits to the great trade routes.

Coal on the Atlantic.

Look again at the map of Canada. We see that it extends from the Atlantic to the Pacific. On the east the peninsula of Nova Scotia stretches far out into the Atlantic.

Nova Scotia is the part of the mainland of America nearest to Europe, where the ports are open all the year round for ships to come and go, and from which railways extend across the continent. It is near the mouth of the St. Lawrence River, along which passes a large trade between Britain and America.

Now, in the northern parts of Nova Scotia, and in the island of **Cape Breton** close adjoining, there are vast deposits of excellent coal.

Here there are abundant supplies of fuel for the growing fleets of steamships which carry on trade across the North Atlantic, for the railways which carry commerce across Canada, for manufacturing and for domestic use.

The coal-fields of Nova Scotia on one side of the Atlantic seem to match those of Britain on the other, and furnish the means for the closest commercial intercourse. Across the North Atlantic, from the United States and Canada, come the greatest supplies of food which the United Kingdom receives from other countries, and for defending this most important of all our food routes in time of war the advantage of having abundant supplies of coal on both sides of the ocean would be very great.

Coal on the North Pacific.

On the western coast of Canada the large island of **Vancouver** stretches out into the Pacific. Between it and the mainland we have an important naval station, and harbours which are fast becoming a centre of trade with the countries which border on the Pacific, India, China, New Zealand, and Australia. On the island of Vancouver are the most important deposits of coal which have yet been discovered along the whole Pacific coast of America. They are as useful for the prosecution and protection of commerce in the North Pacific as those of Nova Scotia are in the North Atlantic.

Again, along the line of the Canadian Pacific Railway, which stretches from Nova Scotia to Vancouver, other extensive beds of coal have been found in the prairie country which lies between the Rocky Mountains and Lake Superior.

These not only furnish abundance of fuel for this almost treeless region, but they are singularly useful as a central point of supply for the great railway which carries merchandise and passengers eastward to the Atlantic, and westward to the Pacific. The shortest route from Britain to Japan and the far East is across Canada, and these three great stores of coal which have been mentioned seem so placed as to offer every facility for speedy intercourse between Europe and Asia.

Coal on the South Pacific.

If now we cross the Pacific, we find the facts connected with the coal supply in Australasia equally interesting and satisfactory.

New Zealand has numerous mines. The quality of the coal varies much in different parts, but that found at **Westport** and **Greymouth**, on the western coast, is considered by the officers of our navy as perhaps the best steaming coal in the world.

H.M.S. Calliope.

In the year 1889 a great hurricane occurred at Samoa, in the Pacific Ocean. All the ships of the United States and German squadrons stationed there were sunk or driven ashore, while the *Calliope*, a British man-of-war, alone escaped by steaming out into the open sea in face of the hurricane. Her commander, Captain Kane, thought that the excellence of the New Zealand coal with which the ship was supplied greatly assisted him in saving her. This circumstance will help us to understand the value of good coal to our ships in these distant and dangerous seas.

In Australia the chief centre of coal supply is around **Newcastle**, in New South Wales. Already about three millions of tons are raised each year from the mines here, which furnish supplies of fuel not only to Australia, but to the ports of the China Seas, and much is even sent across the Pacific to San Francisco and other American ports. Northward, in the province of Queensland, and southward, in the island of Tasmania, important mines have also been opened.

Thus in Australasia our people possess the same advantage of abundant coal to carry on our commerce in the South Pacific and Indian Oceans as they have in the Northern Hemisphere.

Coal in India and South Africa.

A great deal of the coal used at Indian ports has hitherto been brought from England or Australia, but a considerable supply is now being obtained in India itself, while in **Labuan** and **North Borneo** extensive deposits have also been found. In South Africa, too, although no mines have been discovered near the coast, they have been found inland in the colony of Natal and in Rhodesia, and the completion of railway lines has made it possible to bring the coal down to the sea.

Thus we see that our Empire possesses not only stations along the great trade routes where coal may be safely stored for the use of ships, but also large coal-fields at many of the points which seem the most important of all for carrying on trade or protecting it.

Telegraphic Cables.

While we study the vast size of our British Empire we cannot but think how far off are many of the places of which we read. Yet for many purposes the greater part of them are very close indeed to us and to each other.

We all know where the nearest post-office of our village or town is. We go there sometimes to buy stamps, or perhaps to post a letter to some relative in another part of the country, or even in Canada, Australia, India, or South Africa.

If the letter is for any place within these islands, it will probably be delivered on the day we send it, or the day after. If it has to go to Canada, from seven to twelve days will be required to carry it to its destination. If to Australia or New Zealand, the time spent will be between thirty and forty days.

As all the time the letter will be carried along rapidly by rail or steamship, the distances in these last cases will seem still very great.

But the post-office is usually a telegraph-office as well. By paying sixpence we can have a short message sent to most places in the United Kingdom, and in many cases it will be delivered within a few minutes. The wires which go out from the telegraph-office, however, connect us not only with places within these islands, but with most of the remoter parts of the Empire as well. If we are anxious to send a message to Canada or Australia, the East Indies or the West Indies, we can easily do so

if we have the money to pay for the message, and are
willing to spend it.*

Atlantic Cables.

No less than four cables have been laid across the
Atlantic from Ireland to Newfoundland, two from Ireland
to Nova Scotia, and two from England to Nova Scotia.
All these communicate with Canada, the United States,
and other parts of the continent of America.

From Halifax a branch line has been laid to our great
naval station at Bermuda.

Communication is kept up with the West India
Islands through the United States. From Florida lines
of cable extend through all the larger islands, as well as
to Guiana. It is now proposed to extend the line between
Halifax and Bermuda to the West Indian colonies, and
thus the points of connection will be entirely on British
soil.

Eastern Cables.

Next in importance are the lines of communication
with the East. Land lines stretch across Europe in many
directions, and through Asia Minor and Persia to India,
but submarine cables are also laid from England to
Gibraltar, thence through the Mediterranean to Malta,
Alexandria, and Suez, and down the Red Sea to Aden.
From Aden cables giving communication with all parts of

* To Canada the ordinary charge is one shilling per word; to India,
2s. 6d. to 5s. 8d.; to Australia, 2s. 10d. and 3s.; to New Zealand, 3s. 1d.
to 3s. 1d.; to South Africa, 3s. and upwards. These rates are liable to
change at any time. (1895.)

India are laid to **Bombay**, whence, after passing overland to **Madras**, they are continued across the Bay of Bengal to **Penang** and **Singapore**.

From **Singapore** a line extends northward to **Hong-Kong**, where it connects with the telegraph systems of **China**, **Japan**, and **Russia**.

The main line is continued by way of **Java** to **Port Darwin**, in Australia, from which point it crosses the continent to **Adelaide**, and thence to **Melbourne**, **Sydney**, and other points in Australia. From Melbourne connection is made with **Tasmania**, and from Sydney with **New Zealand**.

Cables to the Cape.

Another cable route of importance is that which passes down the **West Coast of Africa** to the **Cape of Good Hope**, thence overland to **Durban**, and up the whole East Coast to Aden, touching at all the more important points in the British, French, German, and Portuguese territories.

The Pacific cable, which was laid in 1903 from **Vancouver** to **Australasia**, has made our British system of cable communication much more complete than it ever was before. The national importance of such a line can scarcely be over-estimated. Before it was completed, all our lines of communication with India and Australasia passed over foreign countries or through shallow seas, where, in the event of a European war, they might be rendered useless. It is believed that this line passing across our own soil in Canada, and through the deep waters of the Pacific Ocean, can be easily guarded and made much more safe in time of war than any which we have hitherto possessed.

In all the great colonies which have been mentioned as connected with Britain by cable, there are no towns of importance, and very few villages even, which have not, just as we have here in these British Islands, their telegraph-office to unite them with the rest of the world.

A very wonderful thing it is to think that over the wires which we see passing out from our village post-office we can send a message to the distant parts and remote corners of this vast Empire which so encircles the globe.

This will make us feel that, after all, the different countries which our people inhabit are in some ways close together.

Another line of cable, not connecting us with other parts of the Empire, but of great value to British commerce, is that which has been laid from England by way of Lisbon, Madeira, and the Cape Verde Islands to the eastern point of South America, whence land lines or submarine cables give connection with all points of importance on that continent.

It is sometimes of great importance to have different routes of telegraphic communication between two points. Here is a striking example, which will also show you what remarkable things can be done by aid of the telegraph.

It may be seen on the map that Suez and Alexandria, in Egypt, are not far apart ; the distance is about 300 miles. When we were engaged in putting down the Egyptian rebellion in 1882, part of our British troops were at Suez and part at Alexandria, and it was most necessary that each should know what the other was doing. The telegraph line between the two places, which is also part of the main line between England and Aden, was broken, probably by the enemy.

It was, however, found possible to send the message by a circuitous route, from Suez to Aden, Bombay, Kurrachee, and across Persia to Constantinople, and so on to London, from which it was telegraphed across France to Marseilles, and then on to Malta and Alexandria.

After travelling 9,000 miles, it arrived at Alexandria only a short time after it left Suez.

NOTE.—There are at present in existence about 125,000 miles of ocean cable. Of these nearly 90,000 miles are owned and managed by British people, leaving only 35,000 miles for all the other nations of the world. Such a fact as this shows how much greater is our interest than that of other nations, in keeping up connection with remote parts of the world.

- - •••

CHAPTER XXIII.

HOW OUR COLONIES ARE GOVERNED.

Self-governing Colonies.

IT has been pointed out that our people in Canada, Australia, Tasmania, Newfoundland, and parts of South Africa are left almost entirely free to manage their own affairs as they wish. They elect the members of their own **Parliaments** or **Legislatures** to make their laws, arrange their taxes, and decide how public money is to be spent.

The King, however, is the head of the Government there, as here, and as he cannot be present in person, a Governor is appointed in each colony to represent him. The Governor has the same power in the colony that the King has here of refusing to assent to any law, but this power is seldom used. Colonies of this kind are said to have *Responsible Government* and to be *Self-governing*.

Crown Colonies.

There is another large class, known as *Crown Colonies*. In these our British Government keeps the control of affairs entirely in its own hands, appointing all public officers: both those who frame the laws and those who carry them out. India is the greatest dependency of this class, which includes a large number of smaller places, such, for example, as Hong-Kong, Gibraltar, and Sierra Leone. Crown colonies are usually either military stations or countries mainly inhabited by other races than our own.

Colonies with Representative Institutions.

A third class consists of those which are said to have *Representative Institutions*. In these the Legislatures which frame laws are partly elected by the people and partly appointed, while the public officers are appointed and controlled by the Home Government. Of this class, Malta, Guiana, and many of the West India Islands may be taken as examples. These colonies usually have a mixed population of blacks and whites.

Almost all the various parts of the Empire of which

we have spoken were, when first occupied, Crown colonies.
But for many years the plan has been pursued of gradually
making colonies self-governing where it is possible so to
do. This commonly depends upon the increase of settlers
of our own race, who are accustomed to self-government.
Thus a Crown colony first obtains representative institutions, and finally responsible government. Colonies maintained chiefly for military or naval purposes, and those with
a very small white population, usually remain in the condition of Crown colonies.

This country's share in the government of the colonies
and dependencies is mainly entrusted to two great Departments of State. At the head of each is one of the King's
Ministers, who must be ready to give account in Parliament for the way in which the work of his department
is done.

The India Office.

The affairs of our vast Indian possessions require the
whole attention of one of these departments—the *India
Office*. At its head is the **Principal Secretary of State** for
India, who is assisted by a council of fifteen members, and
by a large staff of secretaries and clerks.

All directions given to the **Governor General, Governors**,
and other officers who go out to rule India for us, are sent
through the India Office, and it is to the head of the India
Office that these officers make their reports.

The Colonial Office.

The *Colonial Office* deals with the relations of this
country to all the British colonies and dependencies, except

R

India. The Colonial Secretary, who is at the head of it, gives instructions to the Governors whom the King appoints to represent him, receives through them communications from the Legislatures or people of the colonies, and gives information to Parliament about all colonial questions. When we think of the great number of the colonies and dependencies, of the many races who inhabit them, and of the rapid changes through which they are passing, we can readily understand that the Colonial Office has a great many difficult questions to consider and decide.

The Foreign Office.

But a whole class of questions is constantly coming up with which neither the India Office nor the Colonial Office can deal. If a dispute arises between a colony or dependency and any foreign nation, it has to be inquired into and settled by the *Foreign Office*. Many such disputes occur—as, for instance, between Canada and the United States about catching seals in the Behring Sea; between France and Newfoundland about the coast fisheries; between South Africans and Portuguese about the boundaries of their territories.

If we observe what is said in Parliament, or read the Blue Books which tell us what is done at the Foreign Office, we shall find that the Secretary for Foreign Affairs, who is at its head, spends a large part of his time in dealing with colonial questions.

We may see in London, not very far from the Houses of Parliament, the fine buildings of the India Office, the Colonial Office, and the Foreign Office. Should we visit them, we should find hundreds of secretaries and clerks busily engaged on work which concerns the distant parts of the Empire.

These great Departments of State superintend the affairs of the colonies and dependencies under the direction of Parliament. But they can only superintend them; the actual government must be largely entrusted, especially in the Crown colonies and those having representative institutions, to the Governors and other officials who are sent from this country to administer the laws. On the wisdom and justice of these officers often depend the prosperity and happiness of the people they are sent to rule. No other country was ever called upon to send away from its own shores so many able and upright men for the government of distant lands as Great Britain.

How the Colonies are represented in Britain.

If we are in London, and happen to go along Victoria Street, not far from Westminster Abbey, we may notice on the doorways of several of the great buildings there inscriptions such as these :

HIGH COMMISSIONER FOR THE DOMINION OF CANADA.
AGENT-GENERAL FOR VICTORIA.
AGENT GENERAL FOR NEW ZEALAND.

We should understand what these inscriptions mean. All the large self-governing colonies have a great deal of important business to be attended to in Britain, and the colonists are always anxious that their views on public

questions which concern them should be understood by
the Government and people of this country. They therefore send here one of their ablest men who understands
all about the colony which he represents. This **High
Commissioner**, or **Agent-General**, consults with the King's
Ministers about the affairs of his colony, gives information concerning it to emigrants and others, and transacts
its public business in Great Britain. During the last few
years these offices in Victoria Street have gradually become
an important part in the system by which the colonies
are governed.

We now see that the King and his Government are
represented in the colonies by Governors and other officials,
and that the colonies are represented in England by High
Commissioners and Agents-General. Thus colonial affairs
are managed by the united wisdom of our people at home
and those abroad.

The Building of the Empire.

In going round our vast British Empire we have
seen that our people have gained its different parts in
various ways: sometimes by hard fighting with other
nations, sometimes by treaty or purchase, sometimes by
merely occupying lands previously waste or held only by
scattered savage tribes.

But in all cases the conquest has been completed, or
our right to possession established, in other ways. First, it
has been by patient industry, by the toil which clears away
forests, which constructs roads, bridges, and railways,
which makes the soil productive, which changes the

wilderness into a place for happy and comfortable homes. The woodman's axe, the farmer's plough, the miner's pick, the trader's vessel, even more than the sword, have made our nation great and strong.

Again, the Empire has been built up by wise government, by good laws, by securing justice for all, by giving to each the right to possess and enjoy what he has gained by his industry.

We have found that every part of the Empire, however distant, is closely connected by its commerce with these islands. Each colony produces something that people in the United Kingdom want; to every colony we send the products of our mills, workshops, and factories. In proportion to population the colonies are the best customers that the United Kingdom has. The United Kingdom is by far the best customer that colonists have. We are glad to trade with all the world, but it is believed that the Empire could, if necessary, produce everything required for the subsistence and comfort of its people.

In the great colonies there is, as we have seen, abundant space in which industrious people going from this crowded country can find homes. The emigrants who go abroad begin at once to produce things that people in Britain wish to buy, and they themselves begin to want what this country has to sell. Thus those who go and those who stay are kept busy in supplying each other's wants, and so all are made more prosperous and comfortable. So, too, the interests of all become closely linked together. They learn to feel that they are one people.

Now for a people scattered thus all over the world, everywhere engaged in industries, and in exchanging with each other the products of their industries, nothing is so necessary as peace. To secure peace such a nation must be strong, and to be strong the different parts of our Empire must hold together and present a united front to the world. If we do this it is not likely that any enemy would care to attack us.

We know that if a man be good, bent on being just to all around him, willing to help the weak and succour the oppressed, then it is well for the community in which he lives that he should have power, wealth and influence in his hands. So it is with nations. We have a right to be proud of the greatness of our nation, and to build it up still further, if we are resolved that its power shall be used in noble ways. This may be done by dealing fairly with other nations, by ruling wisely and justly the weaker races which have come under our control, by trying to maintain peace in the world. No nation ever had such great opportunities for doing noble work.

"Home."

We have spoken of many links which bind our great Empire together. The strongest of all may be mentioned last. Everywhere abroad where our British people have settled, these islands are spoken of under the tender name of "home." Not only the emigrant, but his children and children's children, speak of coming "home" to England, or Scotland, or Ireland. The great history of our country belongs as much to them as it does to us.

No other mother land has ever had turned towards it so much of affectionate thought. We may well return that affection by trying to understand better and learn more of the new homes which our people have made for themselves beyond the seas.

⁕⁕⁕

> " We sail'd wherever ship could sail,
>   We founded many a mighty state;
> Pray God our greatness may not fail
>   Through craven fears of being great."
>
> *Tennyson.*

INDEX.

Acadians, The, 54
Adelaide, 143
Aden, 198
Africa, 155
..   British Possessions in, 156
..   Climate of, 158
..   Colonisation of, 158
..   South, Climate and products
        of, 161
Agents-General, 259
Albany, 148
Alberta (N. W. T.), 67
Andaman Islands, 230
Annapolis, 75
Anticosti, Island of, 23
Antigua, 87
Arabian Sea, The, 211
Ascension, 185
Asiatic Colonies, 230
Assiniboine R., 66
Athabasca, 67
Atlantic, Routes across, 20
Auckland, 116
Australia, 122
..   Area of, 122
..   compared with Canada,
        124
..   Divisions of, 127
..   First Settlement of, 123
Australian Naval Defence, 140

Bab-el-Mandeb, Strait of, 200
Bahamas, The, 85
Barbadoes, 88
Barrier Reef, The Great, 153
Bass Straits, 118
Basutoland, 174
Bechuanaland, 173
Belfast Lough, 14
Belleisle, Straits of, 22
Bengal, Bay of, 211
Bermuda, 76
Blue Mountains, The (Jamaica), 86
Boers, 160

Bombay, 215
Borneo, British North, 232
Bounty, Mutineers of the, 104
Brahmapootra River, The, 212
Bridgetown (Barbadoes), 88
Brisbane, 149
British Citizenship, 6
British Columbia, 68
..   ..   Products of, 70
British East Africa Company, The
        Imperial, 178
British Empire, Area of, 1
..   ..   described, 1
..   ..   Its Climate, 7
..   ..   Its Common Interests,
                8
..   ..   Its Inhabitants, 7
..   ..   Its Variety, 7
..   ..   Size of, 1
British Guiana, 91
British Honduras, 90
British North Borneo, 232
British Rule in India, 223
British Soldier in India, The, 226
British South Africa Company, 179
" Broken Hill," 143
Brunei, 233
Building of the Empire, The, 260
Burmah, 215
..   Products of, 216
..   Upper, 216

Caicos, 87
Calliope, H.M.S., 249
Canada, Area of, 28
..,   Capital of, 45
..,   Climate, 43
..,   Form of Government, 33, 34
..   History of, 29
..   Maritime Provinces, 47
..   Natural Divisions of, 42
..,   Physical Features of, 36
..,   Political Divisions, 45
..,   Population of, 28

Canada, Railways of, 26
    „   Waterways of, 58
Canadian Emblems, 35
Canadian "Loyalists," 32
Canadian Pacific Railway, 95
Canadian Winter, 44
Canadians, French, 33
Canterbury Plains, N.Z., 111
Cape Coast Castle, 182
Cape Colony, 158
    „   Population of, 160
Caribbean Sea, The, 84
Cattle Trade of United Kingdom, 12
Caymans Islands, 87
Ceylon, 216
    „   Area and Population, 216
    „   Products of, 217
Chaleur Bay, 36
Charlottetown (P. E. I.), 54
Chignecto, Isthmus of, 53
    „   Ship Railway, 52
"Chinook Winds," 44
Chagos Archipelago, 241
Christchurch, 116
Christopher Columbus, 78
Citizenship, British, 6
Civil Service of India, The, 209
Clive, Robert, 206
Coal and Coaling Stations, 245
Coal on the Trade Routes, 246
Coalfields of Australia, 250
    „   „ India, 250
    „   „ Natal, 250
    „   „ New Zealand, 249
    „   „ Nova Scotia, 247
    „   „ Vancouver, 248
Cocos Islands, 232
Cod-fishing off Newfoundland, 75
Colombo, 219
Colonial Office, The, 257
Colonial Secretary, The, 258
Colonies, Crown, 256
    „   Representation of, 258
    „   with Representative Insti-
            tutions, 256
    „   Self-governing, 255
Columbus, Christopher, 78, 86
Confederation, Canadian, 34
Cook Islands, The, 101
Coolie Labour, 82
Cotton, Indian, 215
Crown Colonies, 256
Cruisers, Subsidised Mercantile, 97

Cyprus, 192

Darling Downs, 149
De Beer's Mines, 172
Deccan, The, 215
Delagoa Bay, 179
De Lesseps, M., 193
Demerara, 92
Diamonds (African), 170
Diego Garcia, Island of, 241
Dindings, The, 232
Dominica, 87
Dominion of Canada, 35
Dufferin, Marquis of, 58
Dunedin, 116

East India Company, The, 205
Emigrants and Emigration, 16
Empire, British, Described, 1
    „   „   Area of, 1
Empire, The Building of, 260
    „   Trade of, 211
Empress of India, The Queen de-
        clared, 210
Ensign, The Red, 13
Esquimalt (B. C.), 72

Falkland Islands, 93
Famine in India, 223
Fanning Island, 100
Fiji Islands, 101
Flag, The British, 13
Flags of the Nations, 13
Foreign Office, The, 258
Fredericton, 50
Freetown, 181
French Canadians, 33, 54
French in India, The, 205
"French Shore, The," 74
Fundy, Bay of, 36, 51

Galle, 219
Gambia, 182
Ganges, River, The, 215
Georgetown (Ascension), 185
Gibraltar, 187
    „   Strait of, 189
Gilbert, Sir Humphrey, 74
Gozo, 190
Grenada, 89
Grenadines, The, 88
Griqualand West, 171
Gold Coast, The, 182

Gold in Australia, 135
Guiana, British, 91
Gulf of St. Lawrence, 36
Gulf Stream, The, 20

Habitants, 55
Halifax (Nova Scotia), 22, 23, 48
Halifax and New York, Routes
    Compared, 22
High Commissioner for the Do-
    minion of Canada, 259
Himalaya Mountains, The, 212
Honduras, British, 90
Hong Kong, 234, 235
Hottentots, 160
Hudson Bay, 36, 72
Hudson Bay Company, 73

India, 201
  ,, British Rule in, 223
  ,, Defence of, 219
  ,, Famine in, 223
  ,, Geography of, 211
  ,, Physical Features of, 211
  ,, Population and Area, 201, 203
  ,, Principal Towns of, 214
  ,, Star of, 227
  ,, Trade of, 220
India Office, The, 257
India's Tribute to Britain, 222
Indian Mutiny, The, 209
Indus, The River, 212
Irrigation, Australian, 153
  ,, Indian, 225
" Isle of France," 238

Jamaica, 86

Kaffirs, 160
Kanakas, 151
Kandy, 219
Karroo, The Great, 161
Kerguelen Islands, 155
Khyber Pass, The, 212
Kimberley, 172
King George's Sound, 148
Kingston (Jamaica), 87
  ,, (Ont.), 59

Labrador, 22, 76
Labuan, 233
Lagos, 183
Lakes, Great Canadian, 57

Lancashire, Cotton Trade of, 11
Leeward Islands, The, 87
Liverpool, Commerce of, 11
  ,, Departure from, 10
Logwood, 90
London (Ont.), 59
Londonderry, 15
Louisburg, 47, 48
" Lumbering," 59
Lyttleton, 116

Madras, 215
Mahé, Island of, 240
Mails, The, 15
Malacca, 232
Malay Peninsula, 230
Maldive Islands, 219
Malta, 189
Mandalay, 216
Manitoba, Province of, 65
Maories, The, 109
Maple Sugar, 64
Mashonaland, 179
Mauritius, 238
Mediterranean Sea, The 186
Melbourne, 134
Middle Island (New Zealand), 110
Mohair, 169
Mombasa, 178
Montreal, 56
Montserrat, 88
Mount Morgan Mines, 149
Mutiny, The Indian, 209
Mutton, Frozen, 111

Natal, 172
  ,, Area and Population, 172
  ,, Products of, 172
Native States of India, 228
Naval Defence, Australian, 140
Negroes in West Indies, 83
New Brunswick, 18
Newfoundland, 20, 74
  ,, Fisheries of, 75
New Guinea, 237
New South Wales, 127
New South Wales Wool, 129
New Zealand, 106
  ,, ,, Facts about, 109
  ,, ,, Gold in, 115
  ,, ,, History of, 108
  ,, ,, Middle Island, 110
  ,, ,, Mutton, 112

New Zealand, North Island, 109, 110
,,   ,,   Products of, 111
,,   ,,   Towns and Harbours
                    of, 116
Nevis, 87
Niagara, Falls of, 57
Nicobar Islands, 230
Niger Company, The Royal, 177
Norfolk Island, 104
North Island, New Zealand, 109, 110
North-West Territories (of Canada),
    67
Nova Scotia, 23, 47

Oceanic Empire, The, 3
Ontario, Province of, 56
Orange Free State, The, 175
Orinoco River, 92
Ostrich Farm, A Visit to an, 164
Ostrich Farming, 163
Ottawa, 47

Pacific Coast (of British Columbia),
    69
Pacific, Voyage Across, 98
Panama Canal, 87, 105
Penang, 231
Perim, 200
Perth, 148
Petroleum, 68
Philip, Captain, 128
Pitcairn Island, 104
Plains of Abraham, 31
Plassey, Battle of, 208
Port Castries (St. Lucia), 89
Port Darwin, 145
Port Jackson, 128
Port Said, 195
Portuguese in South Africa, 179
Prince Edward Island, 53
Punjaub, Rivers of, 212

Qu'Appelle River, 67
Quebec, 23, 30, 56
Quebec, Province of, 51
Queen, The, as Head of the Govern-
    ment, 256
Queensland, 148
    ,,   Cattle Runs, 151
    ,,   Products of, 149
Quinine, 218

Rabbits in Australia, 132

Raja Brooke, 233
Raleigh, Sir Walter, 93
Rangoon, 216
Raro-tonga, 101
Red Ensign, The, 13
Red River, 66
Rocky Mountains, 218
Rodrigues, Island of, 240
Routes Across the Atlantic, 20
Royal Naval Reserve, 96

St. Helena, 183
St. John (N. B.), 50
St. John River (N. B.), 49
St. John's, Antigua, 88
St. Kitts Island, 87
St. Lawrence, The, 22
St. Lawrence, Gulf of, 23
St. Lucia, 88
St. Paul's Island, 155
St. Vincent, 89
Salmon, British-Columbian, 71
Sandwich Islands, 101
Sarawak, 233
Saskatchewan River, 67
Self-Governing Colonies, 255
Sepoys, 207
Seychelles, The, 240
Sierra Leone, 181
Singapore, 231
Sikhs, The, 210
Slavery, 80
    ,,   in Africa, 180
Socotra, 200
Soldier, The British, in India, 226
South Australia, 142
    ,,   ,,   Explorers of, 141
    ,,   ,,   Products of, 142
Southern Cross, The, 126
South Georgia, 94
Squatters, 132
Star of India, The, 227
Stewart Island (N. Z.), 110
Straits Settlements, The, 230
Suez, 195
Suez Canal, The, 195
    ,,   Shipping passing through,
            196
    ,,   Value of, 196
Sugar Cane, West Indian, 88
Sugar, Maple, 64
Sunderbunds, The, 213
Suva (Fiji), 103

Swan River, 148
Sydney, 128

Tasman, 118
Tasmania, 118
Tasmanian Products, 119, 121
Tasmanian Wool, 121
Tea, Ceylon and Indian, 217
Telegraphs and Cables, 101, 145, 146, 251
Telegraphic Communication, 5
Temperate Zone, British Possessions in, 105
Thursday Island, 153
Time, Reckoning of, 99
Time throughout the Empire, 100
Tobago, 89
Toronto, 59
Torres Straits, 153
Trade of the Empire, 241
Trade Routes, 212
  „   „   Defence of, 243
Transvaal, The, 175
Trincomalee, 219
Trinidad, 89
Turk's Island, 87

Union Jack, The, 127
United Empire Loyalists, 32
United Kingdom, Size of, 1

Utrecht, Treaty of, 74

Valetta, 192
Vancouver (B.C.), 72, 94, 96
Van Diemen's Land, 118
Vasco da Gama, 158
Victoria, 133
  „   Area of, 133
Victoria (B.C.), 72
Virgin Islands, The, 87
Viti Levu, Island of (Fiji), 103
"Voyageurs," Canadian, 73

Water Carriage, 4
Wattle Trees, 122
Wellesley (Penang), 232
Wellington, 116
Western Australia, 117
West Indies, The, 78
  „   „   Climate of, 79
Windward Islands, The, 88
Winnipeg, Lake, 66
Wolfe, General, Monument to, 30
Wool, New South Wales, 129
Wool, Tasmanian, 121

Yokohama, 96

Zambesia, 179
Zululand, 174

PRINTED BY CASSELL & COMPANY, LIMITED, LA BELLE SAUVAGE, LONDON, E.C.
50.904

www.ingramcontent.com/pod-product-compliance
Lightning Source LLC
Chambersburg PA
CBHW030341270326
41926CB00009B/919